The Key to Inner Peace

by
John H. Hampsch, C.M.F.
with Clint Kelly

D1560260

Performance Press
P.O. Box 7307
Everett, WA 98201-0307

Library of Congress Catalog Number 85-61758

ISBN 0-9613575-2-5

PRINTED IN THE UNITED STATES OF AMERICA

Each volume in the Keyhole Series presents a peek into God's treasure room at the powerful resources available to us, his children. In so doing, we become better equipped to meet the challenges of Christlike living.

Preface

There is a saying that nothing succeeds like success. I'm not sure what that means, but I think it means that one success often leads to another. On the basis of what appears to have been a modest success in the publication of my first book, *Faith: Key To The Heart Of God*, and with the prompting of the readers of that book, I have presumed to publish this present little volume as a somewhat natural extension of the principles delineated in the first book. I have tried to apply those principles of Christ-centered faith to the interior life of prayer and the psychological aspect of dealing with everyday problems that might involve stress-management, anxiety-control, etc. The framework of this study is basically the truths nuggetted in the Word of God.

Each of the six chapters of the book was originally given as an exhortation in a seminar. The transcription and reformulation of the ideas from tape has been the arduous work of my co-author, Mr. Clint Kelly, who did the same with my first book. Mr. Jaime I. Lafosse contributed his expertise in the technical aspects of the production of the book. Permeating all the human endeavor that has gone into this book is the activity of the Holy Spirit, who, I feel, must have worked overtime. May He continue to work in the mind and heart of each reader to inspire and encourage as only He can.

John H. Hampsch, C.M.F

Los Angeles, California
December 8, 1985

TABLE OF CONTENTS

Chapter One:

Authentic Christianity: The Power To Cope

You've no doubt watched television on election night. The returns are in, one candidate concedes defeat and the other rejoices in victory. It is always interesting to me that the victor never uses the occasion of his victory to complain about any lack of cooperation in the campaign or the folks who did not bother to get out and vote.

But the one who went down to defeat, even if by a small margin, has a number of excuses — be it poor advertising, workers not fully committed, lack of understanding by the voters, etc.

It is as if the occasion of victory does not lend itself to complaint. St. Paul reminds us that Christ is *the* Victor, that He has won a great victory for us by His death. He taught the Corinthians (1 Corinthian 15:54) that "death is swallowed up in victory." By His death and resurrection, Christ has won for us a great victory.

If victory does not lend itself to complaint, then there is no room in Christianity for negativism. Christianity is essentially an optimistic way of life. We Christians have access to the supernatural virtue of hope, a sense of happy expectancy.

There have been many definitions of a Christian. Our Lord told us that others would know us by our love. I would add that an authentic Christian, consequently, is one who has the capacity to cope with life and its problems. If Christ is indeed *the* Victor and has already won the victory for us, then what room is there in a Christian's life for defeat? We are "more than victors" (Romans 8:37), "Everyone born of God overcomes the world" (1 John 5:4).

We might call Jesus the Lord of the problematic. We are never really defeated by problems when we are in the Lord. He promised us that when the Holy Spirit is poured out upon us, we will experience *power* — and that includes power to cope with life's difficulties.

When I encounter persons who are totally distraught because of personal problems, surely I feel some sympathy for them. But I realize, too, that they are not availing themselves of the power of Christianity, and therefore are unable to come to grips with life.

There are those, of course, who believe that worry works. They remind me of the wag who protested, "Don't tell me worry doesn't help; most of the things I worry over never happen!"

Worry is useless and accomplishes nothing. Worry gives small things big shadows, distorting reality. Six times Jesus forbade us to worry (Matthew 6:26-34). It shows a lack of trust in God and in no way contributes to our happiness and productivity. To worry about tomorrow is a sure sign that you are unhappy today. You are paying interest before it is due. Chances are it will never come due, but you are out the interest.

Arthur Roach once said that worry is a stream of fear that trickles through the mind cutting a channel into which all our thoughts drain. There is something contagious about worry — it colors all our other thoughts because it creates a negative mentality.

The more I read Scripture, the more I become convinced that an authentic Christian experiences a God-given ability to cope with life, to dispel anxiety before it gains a toehold.

4

It is not so much a matter of trying to delete the problem. There are some naive Christians who feel that because Jesus is the answer to all things, somehow all problems just dissolve in Him. But we are not quite in the vestibule of heaven just yet; we are still in that vale of tears. What this empowerment from God does is give us the ability to cope with the problem — in a sense, to have the pain and not mind it.

This is a paradox we find to one degree in the martyrs like St. Lawrence who sang paeans to God while being burned alive. His pagan executors were baffled as to how anyone undergoing torture and death could be so happy.

A person who is truly in God's Spirit can cope with life's problems because he realizes it is not merely his own doing, but God working through him and with him in divine partnership. He sees, too, by a beautiful insight, the hand of God weaving a mysterious providence through his life. Things ultimately make sense to him. Scripture takes on a rich new meaning, such as Romans 8:37, referring to our victory even in the face of death. Fear of the forces of evil abate when we are fully in the Lord, fully "authentic," or when we have what Paul calls "full maturity in Christ" (Ephesians 3:19).

To be sure, we are always able to improve, to grow beyond today's understanding. No matter how much of God's power we have experienced in our lives, there is more to experience still. There is no point at which we can truthfully say we have reached the limit. Christ said He came to give us life ever more abundantly (John 10:10).

Every one of us can view in our past that which appears to be evil: physical pain, anguish, moral temptations and failures. They did not make much sense then. They seemed wasted years like the 18 years St. Augustine's mother, St. Monica, prayed for her profligate son. Yet the Lord lifted him out of the morass and he became one of the greatest saints in the calendar of saints. God can make good come from hardships or failures (Romans 8:28); that is a facet of His divine ingenuity (cf. Philippians 1:19; James 5:11).

Everything happens for our benefit. That is not to say we passively sit back and take whatever comes. Such quietism is a long-condemned heresy. God wants us to do our part. If we are physically or emotionally ill, we should seek our doctors, psychiatrists and counselors. We ask for miracles, we pray, we use every means possible, natural and supernatural, to change the physical and moral evils in our lives. But we should not become bewildered or discouraged if the change we seek does not come immediately.

In each problematic situation, God offers the power to cope with the problem. "Just as you trusted Christ to save you, so you should trust him also for everyday problems" (Colossians 2:6). That means the act of faith and trust is an ongoing thing, not merely a once-and-for-all acceptance of Christ as Savior. We must reiterate that trust, leaning ever more heavily upon the Lord.

A natural result of this is thanking God and praising Him in the midst of hardship. "In all circumstances give thanks, for this is God's will for you in Christ Jesus" (1 Thessalonians 5:18).

"All circumstances" *includes the things that are hard*. A Christian who has a real sense of God's indwelling within him does not feel abandoned when the storms hit. He is rather one who knows God is present at all times. And he has enough faith (though he does not know *how* God is doing it) to believe that God is working through that difficult situation for that individual's ultimate benefit.

Note that we are to give thanks "*in* all circumstances," not "*for* all circumstances." One doesn't praise God for alcoholism, for pregnancy out of wedlock, for robbery, rape, murder or retardation. But God can be praised for the situations that involve these physical or moral evils, as occasions in which God's providence, mercy and love can be manifested. The deeper our faith and trust, the easier it is to see God's providence, mercy and love in such circumstances. For an "authentic" Christian, any situation in life can be an occasion of praise and thanksgiving to the Lord. Each occasion carries with it a sense of being able to cope with life. But this is true only for what I call "authentic" Christians — "those who love God and are fitting into his plan" (Romans 8:28).

Consequently, although you try to relieve the problems, you do not become distraught should they not be alleviated in the way you planned, for you realize, by faith, the opportunity for grace and the practice of virtue in each situation. Read the remarkable statement of St. James: "Brothers, is your life full of difficulties and trials? Then be happy, for when the way is rough, you patience has a chance to grow . . . When your patience is finally in full bloom, then you will be ready for anything, strong in character, full and complete" (James 1:2-4).

In Romans 5:2-5 Paul says something similar: "We should rejoice when we run into problems and trials, for we know they are good for us. They help us to learn to be patient, and patience develops strength of character in us that helps us trust God more each time we use it until our hope and faith are steady. When that happens, we are able to hold our heads high no matter what happens to us and know that all is well for we know how dearly God loves us. We feel this warm love everywhere within us because God has given us his Holy Spirit of love to fill our hearts with his love."

Along with faith and hope, Paul placed great emphasis on love, interweaving it with the growth of patience, because all the virtues are tied together. As St. Thomas Aquinas said, "You don't grow your hand one finger at a time. All the fingers grow simultaneously." A life of virtue grows likewise.

We can grow in patience, hope, trust, love and faith, but we do it most effectively in the context of suffering. Not that we should cling to the suffering as an end in itself. There is a right and wrong concept of victimhood. Paul said, "I beseech you, brethren, present yourselves as living sacrifices, holy and pleasing to God" (Romans 12:1). At the same time we must have a constant awareness that God is there, eager to remove the problem, or give us the strength to bear it. To be disconsolate in suffering is to show that God's role in that situation is not recognized or appreciated.

Sometimes enormous good comes from suffering and evil. There is a long chain of providential circumstances linking all of human history, but within the life of each individual there is that same intricate thread of God's involvement. We must learn to recognize it, and when we do, through that insight that comes with the presence of God's Spirit within us, we attain a continual calm awareness that God is working his loving providence in every event of our lives.

Paul said where evil abounds, let grace abound more (Romans 12:21). God is there. What is not always there is our awareness of that God-presence weaving its pattern in the midst of evil, suffering, hardship, etc. A strength to cope with the problems and misadventures of life comes with that awareness.

So, then, why do we feel so helpless? We say, Lord, I pray, but I don't hear an answer; things keep getting worse and worse. Lord, why don't you do it my way? We tell God how to run things. Paul's approach shows deeper insight. While saying that we should praise God in all things that happen to us, in Philippians 1:3 and II Thessalonians 1:4 he says, "My prayer for all of you is full of praise to God." This praise prayer was *because of* the patience and faith they displayed under persecution.

Instead of saying that he prayed for their relief from problems, he praised God for their reaction to the trials. He thanked God because they allowed God's plan to be worked out in their lives in the midst of hardship.

In chapter 16 of Acts we read about Paul's imprisonment in Philippi and Macedonia. His attitude of victoriousness went before him. The people heard about how the Lord was working through him. To make doubly certain Paul stayed incarcerated, his captors placed him in a subterranean prison, shackled him to the floor, stationed guards outside who had been threatened with death should he escape. We know how the power of God worked in this adverse situation, enabling Paul to

8

convert his jailer. *God didn't immediately solve the problem of Paul's imprisonment, but He enabled Paul to cope with the problem in joy and used the problem to bring about a providential conversion.* God solved the problem only later by freeing Paul when the earthquake jarred the prison doors open.

God is there, whether to help us solve the problem or to bear it, allowing good to result from it: "I want you to know this, dear brothers, everything that has happened to me here has been a great boost in getting out the good news concerning Christ. For everyone around here, including all the soldiers over at the barracks, knows that I am in chains simply because I am a Christian, and because of my imprisonment many of the Christians here seem to have lost their fear of chains. My patience has encouraged them and they have become more and more bold about telling others of Christ" (Philippians 1:12-14).

God used Paul to give courage to others and they in turn by their chains and suffering gave courage to still more. A proliferation of courage, the power of God acting through divine providence in the midst of suffering. This holds true whether it's a matter of narcotics addiction or alcoholism or poverty or cancer or arthritis, *God is there working through us.* Sometimes He is glorified through a cure; other times He works more subtly. But in the life of a loving "authentic" Christian, what appears to be a failure, evil, is really used by God to bring about good.

Every Christian ought to be in the position where he has a greater capacity to give witness than the need to receive it. He is so strong in the Lord that he can walk through life bearing enormous burdens relatively easily. Others will ask how he can be so happy, so self-contained.

Everyone needs to hear witness, of course, but ask yourself which position you are in. Are you the kind who needs to be lifted up *because of your weakness,* or the kind who has opened yourself so thoroughly to the God-presence of Jesus' spirit within you that your very life gives witness and praise to the Lord in the eyes of others.

It's not bad to be on either side of the fence. But you will grow more in the Spirit if you are giving witness rather than in need of witness to encourage you.

When church-goers are grumblers and complainers, they really have not learned the lesson that Christ is the Victor — that everything comes under His power when we are immersed in Him. "Neither can you bear fruit unless you remain in me" (John 15:4).

There are people who say they can be resigned to God for air pollution, traffic jams, inclement weather, a lost job or a terminal physical illness, but not for an unwed pregnant daughter or a son on narcotics. They partition the events in their lives, as if this compartment contains things in God's plan, but this other one does not. But God says *everything* fits in His will, even evil (only permissively, of course). Those who commit evil will have to render an account to God, but the evil that men do fits in His permissive will, and ultimately good can come from it. For those who love God *all things* work together for good — sometimes in mysterious ways, yes; and this provides a tremendous challenge to our faith, as we surrender to the Lord and admit that while it may not make sense to us, it makes perfect sense to God.

Job was a very holy man, a millionaire of the Orient whom God levelled to the ground. In utter devastation, he was a man all but destroyed, yet one who could say, "The Lord giveth, the Lord taketh away, blessed be the name of the Lord." Yet the Lord argued with him and questioned him as to whether he really accepted God's wise and loving providence. Job confesses (chapter 42) that he has indeed foolishly denied God's providence. Only then was he restored in health and family, wealthier than ever before.

The greatest lesson lay within that last chapter of the book of Job — that God is there in the midst of every event of life (cf. James 5:11). The only ones who can recognize His loving presence in difficult situations are those with deep faith. The deeper, more intimately we allow God to operate within our lives, the better able we are to cope with life. Nothing perturbs a godly person. *Nothing!* Read Psalm 37:39-40.

The gift of faith empowers you to get a spiritual grip on life. We will hear of wars and rumors of wars, raging crime and rampant terrorism, and *still* we will be able to walk this vale of tears with our head held high because "we feel his warmth within us from the Holy Spirit that fills our hearts with his love" (Romans 5:5).

As it says in the book of Ecclesiastes, life is a thrilling adventure. We should face it squarely and use it, enjoy the good things of life as long as they are not sinful, and when the hardships come, realize that they are equally from the hand of God. Praise and bless God for them.

Should feelings of dereliction and bewilderment beset you in the troubled times, take hold of the living Word of God. Make Romans 8:35-39 your prayer of victory:

"Who can ever keep Christ's love from us? When we have trouble or calamity, when we hunted down or destroyed, is it because he does not love us anymore? If we are hungry, or penniless or in danger, threatened with death, has God deserted us? No. For the scripture tells us for his sake we must be willing to face death every day. Despite all this, overwhelming victory is ours through Christ who loved us enough to die for us. I am convinced that nothing can ever separate us from his love. Death can't, life can't, the angels won't. All the powers of hell itself cannot keep God's love away. Our fears for today, our worries about tomorrow, or wherever we are high above the skies or deep in the deepest oceans, nothing will be able to separate us from the love of God demonstrated in our Lord Jesus Christ."

Taking a Second Look at Authentic Christianity: The Power To Cope

Ask Yourself (Or discuss with a study group) . . .

1. Why is Christianity said to be an optimistic form of religion?

2. Define the term "authentic Christian."

3. What is it about worry that is so damaging?

4. Is Christianity trouble-free? Why or why not?

5. What situations in your life have demonstrated God's ability to cause good to come from evil?

6. What are the right and wrong concepts of victimhood?

7. Explain St. Paul's reputation for victoriousness. How did it advance the Gospel?

8. Why is it wrong to partition events in our lives into those within God's will and those outside His will?

9. Is giving thanks in all things coping, or copping out? Explain.

10. In what ways are problems good for us?

Chapter Two:

Scriptural
Problem-Solving:
How To Cope

The old bromide says, "Think big, raise elephants." There are certain things in life for which we have to think big: home, family, career. But we have to train ourselves to think small in other matters. God is concerned about some very small things, such as the number of hairs on our heads (Matthew 10:30). A trivial fact to us, perhaps, but St. Matthew reminds us it is of importance to the Lord.

One crucial matter in which we have to "think small" is in regard to our problems.

Think of some circumstances in the space and time in which we find ourselves. For example, we speak of the hugeness of our world, some 25,000 miles in circumference. Crossing the country by plane, one can see vast, unoccupied territories. In Alaska, I have gone 300 to 400 miles without seeing a single human inhabitant.

Or think of outer space full of unknown worlds and uncharted galaxies.

Yet your world, your immediate environment, is not in outer space. Few of us call wilderness home. At any given moment within your house, neighborhood or church, you are part of a very small and limited world that is actually yours.

Think in terms of the billions of people on earth and how you have contact with but a tiny fraction of them. Consider the distant future of an eternal life ahead of you. You are living but a split second at a time. You are not living the last minute or the next minute; you are living now, this minute.

In realilty we have a small world, a small number of people in that world, a small period of time with which to cope. In that sense, we can and should think small. When life becomes a fearful strain, we need to cut it down to its real size to effectively cope with it. It is this time, these people, the here and now that I must deal with. This I can handle for today.

The old aphorism says, "By the yard, life is hard; by the inch, life's a cinch." If we take life in too big a chunk, we can't handle it. Alcoholics Anonymous policy embraces this principle. To tell an alcoholic that he can never take a drink the rest of his life is to impose a nearly impossible demand. But tell him to resolve not to drink today, and then reassess tomorrow; that seems not only reasonable but manageable. Take life an inch at a time and you can cope.

God does not gloat over our sufferings, though His will permits them. God controls our suffering. Christ, suffering in the Garden of Gethsemane, turned to His own Father and prayed, "If it is possible, let this chalice of pain and suffering pass from me." God the Father has the control. But we must never pray Christ's prayer ourselves without adding His follow-up statement: "Not my (human) will, but your (divine) will be done."

In shrinking our problems down to manageable size, let's think of hardships and suffering in two general categories: those which are unnecessary and those which are inescapable.

You'd be surprised how much of your life is unnecessary suffering, exaggerated problems. A large percentage of people are problem oriented. Their entire lives are geared to thinking about troubles; they are consumed with worry about health, job, children, etc. The majority of their waking life is problem-geared. It is a morbid, gloomy emotional state. For the vast majority, such preoccupation is totally unnecessary. They are quick to place the blame on God for their "inconsiderate" children or their "unresponsive" mates, when in fact they are fomenting the problem themselves.

Perhaps nine-tenths of all counseling clients really do not want consultation, but consolation. Rather than consultation, they seek reinforcement of their own self-pity. They are not in search of a solution to their problems, preferring instead to cling to them. I often wonder what would happen if God one day gave us a Garden of Eden, a problem-free paradise to live in. Many persons, I think, would be truly disturbed because they wouldn't have anything to worry about or talk about!

Of course there is much to be said for sympathy, empathy and consolation. God expects us who give Christian counsel to be good shepherds and offer a word of support. But suffering that many tend to exaggerate, harp upon and are morbidly preoccupied with, and never lay at the feet of the God of consolation, is a needlessly heightened suffering. There can be no victory in it.

Persons who are deeply Spirit-filled are very aware of Paul's words in Romans 8:26, "By faith the Spirit helps us in all of our daily problems (weakness)." The person who never relates a daily problem to the Holy Spirit is out of accord with the same Spirit. Such a one is trying to hack a way up the mountain of life. Why endure such an arduous journey when God invites us to reach out and take His hand and walk the rocky path with His help and guidance?

Paul goes on to say that the Spirit will help us even in our praying so that when we do not know how to pray or what to pray for, the Holy Spirit will take over and speak for us in the heavenly realms. If our problems have us stymied beyond words, God has made provision for even that! Whether or not we have access to a sympathetic human confidante (a real boon!), we always have access to the Master who loves and understands us *beyond human comprehension.*

In order to place our problems in God's lap, we must learn how to let go of them. To stop clinging to hardships, stop viewing them through a magnifying glass. When we take a difficulty and blow it out of all proportion, at that point we fail to see it from God's point of view.

St. Peter put the matter succinctly: "Cast your anxieties upon the Lord, for he cares for you" (I Peter 5:7). Take your problems and dump them in God's lap. If you are constantly taking them out and studying their every morbid nuance, you are not looking at them as God does.

There was an old Arab whose tent was pitched next to a company of Whirling Dervishes. Someone asked him if his neighbors bothered him. He said no. When asked what he did about them, he replied, "I let them whirl."

Sometimes we have to allow the problems of life to simply whirl around us and not disturb us. A fly buzzing around your head could drive you to distraction if you allowed it to, but not if you *choose* to ignore it. Over-preoccupation with the tiniest annoyance can render you powerless in living out God's plan for you. Do not become obssessed with the "flies."

For example, take the futility of attempting to please everyone. A political leader who would take every criticism to heart would be unable to function. We must not let problems and opposition hurt us, but rather must desensitize ourselves to them, all the while growing in sensitivity to God's will.

There are an amazing number of people who believe that other people can hurt them in nonphysical ways. But you can choose to refuse to become poisoned by your own hypersensitivity.

This earth is enveloped in a heavy atmosphere. When a meteor comes hurtling through space and strikes that atmosphere, a "falling star" is formed and can be seen if it occurs at night. The heat of the friction with our atmosphere causes the meteor to be burned up, destroyed. It is a rare thing for a meteor to hit the earth (and thus become a meteorite). The atmostphere, then, is the earth's protective cushion.

We have to be within an atmosphere of God's love, that protective cushion against the onslaughts of life, in order to be victorious Christians. We need to "put on Christ" (Romans 13:14). The deeper we grow in the life of the Spirit, the more fully we are within the protective covering of God's love (Psalm 61:3). The more enveloped we become in that love, the more invulnerable we become to the destructive forces that would otherwise destroy us.

Everything that happens to us redounds to our benefit (Genesis 50:20; Hebrews 12:10-11). We *"know"* this, Paul affirms (Romans 8:28), as an expression of faith-spawned certitude. That means pain, suffering, rejection, false accusations, surly kids and an uncommunicative spouse must be viewed in the same light as a steady paycheck, choice lake-front property, or a year without dental bills! A person lacking *faith* will lack also *hope*, and not see adversity as potentially beneficial, will not be open to the *love* of God inherent in this scriptural promise of divine aid. Faith works through love (Galatians 5:6). We have to have the faith to believe that God's tender love will cushion us from the meteor impacts of life.

The Council of Trent in 1545 proclaimed that faith is the basis and root of our justification and our sanctification. Not just our salvation, but our growth in holiness. Without faith, we go nowhere.

I once allowed myself to be hurt by a person and it changed my whole life. My religious superior came into my room at the seminary years ago and said, "You are a very poor religious with no sense of your vow of poverty," as he pointed to a plastic cover over a light switch that I had purchased for 10 cents to protect the wall from fingerprints. He spent 15 minutes ranting over my spiritual destitution represented by my purchase of that 10 cent switch plate cover.

I did not make reply, but lay awake that night for two hours chewing on the "chewing-out" I had received. Then it dawned on me how stupid it was for me to allow someone to interfere with my happiness (and my sleep). How could I brood over something this small and allow my happiness to be disturbed? I recalled Seneca's words that "anyone stupid enough to allow others' opinions of him to make him unhappy, deserves to be unhappy because of such stupidity." I resolved then, with God's help, to never again allow anyone to shake me like that, but to live in God's love, while not ignoring others' helpful criticisms of my faults.

Since then, thanks be to God, no one has ever disturbed me that way. With God's help, anyone can do the same.

As effective Christians, we can live invulnerably in some senses of that word. That does not mean without suffering. It does mean without *unnecessary* suffering, which is the vast majority of the suffering we experience. Turn a deaf ear to those who would hurt you. You can, if you open yourself to the gift of God's loving acceptance. He will never alienate, reject or deprive us of His love, therefore we need never unduly concern ourselves with human manifestations of alienation, rejection, or lack of love.

But what about unavoidable suffering? The inescapable circumstances that threaten our well-being? We must learn how to *accept* them. There is little we can do to change the weather, the price of meat at the supermarket or our spouse's personality. We must recognize our limits to change our environment.

Finding a shoulder to cry on may offer release for the moment, but in itself does not get at the root of the problem. We may need friends, support and aspirin to relieve the symptoms, but let us not kid ourselves into believing that they in themselves can solve the problems.

To find the right perspective on inescapable suffering, then, we have to turn to something far more radical — divine providence, the mind of God. If we do not, we wallow in self-pity and may even rail at God. We try various home remedies. One is blaming others: "I wouldn't drink so much if my wife didn't nag me so much." Or we sit and brood. Sometimes we corner others to inform them that "nobody knows the trouble I've seen." And we end up in a "pity party."

Home remedies may produce some temporary, superficial satisfaction. But we know we're still just taking aspirin for a brain tumor. Ultimately, everyone we touch becomes miserable along with us, as our moaning "drains" them.

Unable to solve a problem, we must learn to live with it. Acceptance. It's such a simple thing most people don't try it, even when they're desperate. Their approach seems to be, "If all else fails, follow directions." Yet, as we have seen, the Bible directs us to lean on God. For too many professing Christians, it is the last resort, not the first resort.

We cannot, however, be Christians *and* fatalists. We must not say "There's nothing I can do about it, so I will do nothing." God expects us to care for our health and other needs to the best of our ability. Yet we need to seek His wisdom to know the difference between what we can and can't change, and to know how to proceed. God commended Solomon for seeking wisdom first. Enormous wealth was God's bonus to Solomon because he sought after righteousness and understanding *first* (I Kings 3:9); he wanted first to follow God's will in problems he was to face — as the decision regarding the two prostitute mothers (verses 16-28).

The whole "theology of the problematic" has been summarized in the prayer of St. Francis de Sales (reformulated by Niebuhr), the great serenity prayer: "Lord, grant me the *serenity to accept* what I cannot change, but give me the *courage to change* what I can, and the *wisdom to know* the difference."

Those who continually complain, feeling helpless and frustrated; those who wallow in self-pity are overwhelmed by their circumstances rather than become masters of them. *Seek* God's wisdom first, *ask* for the serenity to effectively cope with life, and He will keep you on an even keel. You will then be equipped to change the things you can and accepting of the things you can't.

God does not want us to simply tolerate suffering. "Offering it up" in passive resignation is not good theology, despite what our religion teachers taught us.

Instead, we should ask to receive a change. "Ask the Father anything in my name believing and it will be given you." Christ reminds us His Father and ours wants to give gifts to those who do His will. One of His gifts is simply freeing us of our problems or lightening of our burdens. "My yoke is sweet, my burden light" (Matthew 11:30). Burdens are something we can change with His help. We can pray for miracles and direction by divine providence. That is not passive acceptance. It is un-ruffled acceptance of *unavoidable* suffering while pursuing divine action to change *avoidable* suffering.

In Colossians 2:6 Paul says, "Just as you trusted Christ to save you, trust him, too, for each day's problems. Let your roots grow down into him and draw up nourishment from him. See that you keep on growing in him and become strong and vigorous in the truth you were taught. Let your lives overflow with joy and thanksgiving for all he has done."

We miss these precious gems. We spend hours in dead-end trips trying to find solutions to our problems when God has already given us solutions! One of these is the simple realization that God brings good out of evil — an oft-repeated trick of divine ingenuity. "He understands us and knows what is best for us *at all times*" is one paraphrase of Ephesians 1:8. Everything that happens, happens to our *benefit*.

Christ was a victim of injustice and He accepted the injustice in being crucified. It was remotely through that very injustice that we were saved. Everything that was done to Him was permitted by the will of the Father for our salvation (Ephesians 1:4-5). How does that compare with how we handle our problems and injustices against us? We would, if we could, escape unbearable situations, but we cannot. Christ, on the other hand, could have escaped, but did not. He said He freely chose to lay down His own life, they did not really take it from Him forcibly (John 10:18).

Christ's Gethsemane prayer was answered in the Resurrection. That He had to first suffer the crucifixion did not deter Him from redeeming us. That is the Christic mentality that we need in our acceptance of suffering.

Is our own life Christ-patterned? "If they have persecuted me, they will also persecute you." To gird us for such hardship, He tells us first to pray, "Thy will be done," to submit our wills to God's. Then He says to put our priorities in order. "Seek first the kingdom of God and his holiness and all these other things you're seeking will be given you" (Matthew 6:33). If we spent as much time in seeking God's will, His kingdom and holiness, as we do morbidly brooding over our petty problems, we would be saints. How much time do we spend glorifying God *in* our problems, following this Christ-designed scenario?

All events in our life in some mysterious way are marvelously orchestrated just as they are in nature. There is an ecological balance between the amount of carbon dioxide given off by plants and the carbon dioxide needed to maintain life in the oceans. Our own planet is perfectly distanced from the sun to sustain an incredible variety of life forms. And so it is in the events of human interaction. Everything is orchestrated. Another person hurts you, but from that good comes. Perhaps in such an event you are the cause of grace that brings that individual to salvation, and God receives the glory. Or through such an event you grow in faith, fortitude or patience (James 1:2-4; Romans 5:3-5).

This in some way is the living metabolism of the cosmic Christ that De Chardin speaks about, based on Paul's remark in Ephesians 4:10, "Jesus fills all things everywhere with himself." *There is no place or situation or problem where Christ is not present* (Colossians 1:17). Do our lives reflect the truth of that statement or do we put the lie to Scripture by living a life of defeat and negativism?

God wants us to be happy here on earth. It is not all to be a vale of tears. But we often refuse to look where God is pointing. Confucius said happiness does not consist in having what you want, but in wanting what you have.

How do you go about wanting what you have? Place

it in the context of our Christian "Thy will be done" prayer. Do you really want what God wants? If so, then want what has happened in your life (at least the unavoidable). Genuine happiness is not found in freedom from want or pain, but in freely conforming our will to God's will, wanting what He wants.

Going from one drug to another, from one bar to another, from one prostitute to another, are nothing but frenetic attempts to find a temporary, false happiness. It cannot last, it will not last, because such shallow pleasure-seeking is not true happiness-seeking, and not in the context of God's will. People of that genre are striking matches in the darkness instead of turning on the light switch for the lasting glow from God that illuminates the way to eternal happiness.

When we come into the dimension of genuine growth in Christ, we can perceive a change in our mentality, a different attitude towards our problems. We come to know that self-gratification is like the King Midas touch that does not last.

God never gives us too much to bear. He measures each cross to fit. One size does not fit all. You may have a cross that's too big for me to carry, or mine may be too much for you. Rest assured that all have been designed with the bearers in mind. Whether it means bodily aches and pains, spiritual twinges or mental anguish, the way of the cross doesn't stop at the cross but at the open tomb.

We must get beyond the material, and our immaturity, to experience life from God's point of view. A baby is very discontent when its mother takes away a sharp knife it's been playing with. The mother's love for that child tells her to "hurt" it by taking that prized knife away in order to spare it physical injury. Her love replaces the knife with something better, a rattle or bottle.

Each of us is as a little child wanting God to take the cancer away. Perhaps His reply is often no, you will die of that cancer. What we do not know is that a thousand souls on the brink of hell may be given the grace of a death-bed repentance and salvation because of the intercessory value of our suffering while resigned to

God's will (cf. Colossians 1:24). If we understood that, we would see that God loves us so much that He is letting us become "redeemers" with a small "r" as Bishop Sheen used to say. In our truth-distorting anguish, we accuse Him of not loving us, of not answering the bell of our prayers when we ring.

Our petty minds accuse God of mismanaging the universe. To be sure, God's ways are often inscrutable (Isaiah 55:8-9), but never are they misguided (Job 37:14-24). He wants us to do what we can to get free of our suffering and give glory to Him by that means. But should the release from the problem come late or never, we must learn to give Him glory in the midst of the problem.

Everything in life has a good side. You can visit the city dump and rejoice at being reminded of your gift of having a sense of smell. How about the cat that's yowling outside your window at three in the morning? Praise God for your sense of hearing, because if you couldn't hear the cat, you couldn't hear a symphony. You can place everything in a good light and often humor-spangled: Good Pope John when asked how many men worked in the Vatican replied, "About half."

God will allow us to look over His shoulder at the blueprint He has for us. But first we need to stop feeling sorry for ourselves, to wake up in the morning with a "Yes, Lord, what would you have me do for you today?" Otherwise we will never feel the cleansing action of God's grace, because He will be unable to get through to us.

If you saw a naked baby lying in the snow, you simply could not walk past and ignore it. You'd pick it up, care for it and try to sustain its life. The very helplessness of that infant demands it. If we present ourselves as weak, helpless babies, naked, lying in the snow, God cannot resist catching us up in His loving arms and pressing us to His Sacred Heart. He loves us, wants good for us, desires our comfort, longs to do things for us.

Our problems have to be seen from a God's-eye view. With that perspective it would be easy to "let go, let

God." How many of our problems would dissolve today if we allowed God to take the controls of our life? And the few problems that wouldn't dissolve would be gratefully accepted as distasteful, but life-saving, health-giving medicine.

Taking a Second Look at Scriptural Problem-Solving: How To Cope

Ask Yourself (Or discuss with a study group) . . .

1. How and why should we "think small" about life's problems?

2. What kinds of suffering are unnecessary, and why?

3. What is the essential difference between the way you view your problems and God's view?

4. Why are "home remedies" ineffective when faced with inescapable suffering?

5. How does seeking God's wisdom enable us to cope with unavoidable suffering?

6. What does Christ's acceptance of injustice teach us about coping with problems?

7. What proof do we have that events of our lives are orchestrated by God for our good?

8. Why do we often accuse God of mismanaging our lives? What is really happening?

9. What part do "silver linings" play in our Christianity?

10. Examine one personal problem in your own life from a new perspective in light of the insights proposed in this chapter.

Chapter Three:

Peace Of The Cross: Heroism Made Easier

There once was a man who went to the health department to complain about the unsanitary conditions he was living in. He said, "You've got to do something about this. I'm living with my five brothers in one room and they have 10 dogs and 12 monkeys in the same room. The air is stifling, it's nearly impossible to breathe, you must do something!"

The health department official replied, "Well, first of all, why don't you open a window?"

"What?" asked the unhappy man incredulously, "and lose all my pigeons?"

Sometimes we compound our suffering unwittingly. We don't realize that we do have some control over the sufferings we inevitably face in everyday life.

One of the ways we can learn to cope with suffering is by learning to attain and maintain an interior peace in the midst of our sufferings. Once we have acquired that divine art of maintaining peace, expecially letting God's peace abide within us (John 14:27), and then live it in a very real way, we will find that the cross itself is not so hard, that if it is heavy, we have the strength to bear it.

I want to give you a scriptural plan, a guide to mastering the art of maintaining peace in the midst of suffering. I want to show you how to minimize your sufferings by maximizing your peace in those sufferings.

First, we must acknowledge the problems we have before the Lord, not to just turn to Him in self-pity. Second, we must become totally objective about the problem itself, able to see it in the proper perspective, that of eternity. Third, we must be able to pray that we attain this peace in our affliction — not simply pray for the removal of the problem itself. Fourth, we must trust in God to fulfill His promises to help us in our sufferings. Fifth, we must be truly immersed in the Word of God to receive the power to sustain the cross. Sixth, we must be docile or teachable regarding God's will when suffering afflicts us, especially when it is God's form of discipline to correct and train us.

Afterwards, then, God is going to either remove our cross completely and answer our prayer in the way in which we'd hoped, or He will give us the strength to bear it joyfully. We need to know what to do in either case.

Make a mental effort as we discuss each of these steps in turn to apply them to yourself in the context of the problems you are now experiencing.

Acknowledge the Problem

We must acknowledge the problem before the Lord. Implied is a dependence upon the Lord for help. That kind of prayer is something of a lamentation prayer. In the scriptural book of Lamentations we find this reference: "I was broken-hearted" — depressed — "and in despair with guilt feelings. I'm afraid of crime around me, afraid of sickness, afraid of death."(1:20). Can you identify with some of those things? That is the acknowledgement.

In Psalm 25:16-17, David acknowledges this: "I am helpless, Lord. I'm overwhelmed, in deep distress. My problems seem to go from bad to worse. Save me from them, O Lord."

Or perhaps you can identify with II Corinthians 6:4, where Paul says he had suffered hardship of every kind, been beaten, jailed, worked to exhaustion, faced angry mobs, spent sleepless nights watching, and gone hungry. Or you may be mature enought to identify with his insights in II Corinthians 4:8-18: "We are pressed on every side by troubles, but we are not crushed; we are perplexed because we do not know why things happen as they do. But we don't give up and quit. We are hunted down, but God never abandons us. We get knocked down but we get up and keep going. These bodies of ours are constantly facing death just as Jesus did, so it is clear to all that it is only the living Christ within us who keeps us safe. Hence we are in constant danger for our lives because we serve the Lord, but this gives us constant opportunities to show forth the power of Jesus Christ. We boldly say what we believe, trusting God to care for us. That's why we never give up. Though our bodies are dying, our inner strength in the Lord is growing every day. These troubles and sufferings of ours, after all, are quite small and don't last very long and yet this short time of distress will result in God's richest blessings upon us forever and ever. So we do not look at what we can see right now — the troubles all around us; we look forward to the joys in heaven which we have not seen. The troubles will soon be over but the joys to come will last forever."

Be Objective

Persons who are depressed and filled with anxieties are persons who are inevitably problem-oriented individuals. Much of their psychic energies are focused on problems and they become introverted people. As a result, they tend to exaggerate their own sufferings. Their problems seem to occupy the majority of their free mental time. Their minds spontaneously gravitate back to their problems. We often call then worrywarts.

To get these people to be objective, they have to be pulled out of themselves. The Bible tells us how to be objective. One sentence from the previous passage is a good start: "This *short* time of distress will result in God's richest blessings forever and ever." Even if you live to be a hundred years old and you have suffered pain the entire way, it is still just a flash in eternity.

To help place that in perspective, read I Peter 1:6, "Be truly glad; there is a wonderful joy ahead, even though the going is rough for awhile down here." Or I Peter 5:10, "After you've suffered a *little while*, our God, who is full of kindness, through Christ will give you his *eternal* glory." And in Romans 8:18, Paul says, "What we suffer now is nothing compared to the reward — the glory — that is to come." Again, in Galatians 6:9 he says, "After a while we will harvest the blessings *if* we don't get discouraged and give up."

Look at the whole constellation of problems in your life, together and individually, and apply this to yourself. Part of the reward is going to be precisely *for* that suffering, but it has to be suffering that is not wasted. It must be done in Christ.

Suppose I were to ask you to let me prick your finger with a pin. You refuse. But, I say, I'll give you a nickel if you let me do it. Again, you refuse. But suppose I offered you a million dollars a year for the rest of your life if you allowed me to prick your finger with a pin? Undoubtedly you would eagerly say, "Of course, of course, here, here!"

Why would you refuse in one situation and accept in the other? The answer may appear obvious, but if you put it into a philosophical context, the real answer is that there is a total disproportion between the suffering — the pin prick — and the reward. That's what Scripture refers to when it speaks of the "hundredfold." That's what Paul means when he says that the sufferings of this life cannot compare (because they are so disproportionate) to the glory that is to come.

St. Theresa is said to have appeared after her death to one of her fellow religious and to have said that no human words can describe the reward that is given for picking up even a lowly straw, when it is done for love of God. Of how much more value is *suffering* when it is Christ-centered (I Peter 4:13)?

It takes faith to believe that whatever sufferings you have now will be incredibly rewarded; that the worst suffering that is possible to experience in this life is but a pinprick by comparison to the treasures of heaven. If only we could see this from the viewpoint to eternity 10 million years from now. We'd look back upon earth, see our little sufferings and wonder how we could have complained so. We will stand amazed at all the extra glory we have received because of that tiny suffering. We will be staggered by the greatness of God. How could we have missed what the Bible says so plainly about suffering and inner peace?

That is what I mean by objectivizing the problem, viewing it from the perspective of eternity, gaining a God's-eye-view of the matter. We possess a severly limited worm's-eye-view. It takes a certain greatness, a certain magnanimity, to transcend ourselves, to get above it and see, by faith, what that problem *really* is, and to see God's plan in it. Blessed are those who do not see and yet believe, Jesus said to Thomas (John 20:29). There is a very obvious role of *faith* in suffering to bring about a corresponding *peace* in suffering.

Someone has said that life is like a grindstone — it will either grind you down or polish you up. It can destroy you or make a hero out of you. Every suffering is either a stumbling block or a stepping-stone, depending upon how you use it.

Some people shake their fists at God. They accuse Him of being loveless for allowing suffering. Kindergarten Christians do not see that God often sends diamonds wrapped in brown paper sacks. Through lack of faith in this truth, the diamonds are tossed aside by persons who don't see the precious gift that God conceals within that cross. Wrapped up in their self-pity, their only consolation is that same self-pity. Instead of being objective, they are utterly subjective. They dwell on the arthritis pain in their shoulder, never comprehending that 40,000 people die of starvation every day — it's not their problem. The only real problem in their life's tiny microcosm is the pain in their shoulder.

To become objective, we need magnanimity (one of the 56 virtues in the catalog of virtues). Magnanimity means "greatness of soul." Suffering, if properly used, results in greatness of soul; suffering, if improperly used, results in shriveling of the soul, in petty, twisted, griping, morbid, picayune individuals.

Sometimes the more testing we get, the more blessing we receive — as long as sufferings are used as stepping-stones, not stumbling blocks. We become richer for the test, the trials, the temptations. Tests make us more fruitful, more secure. Ask anyone who works for NASA. Testing in technology is essential. God, too, gives us tests. He needs to try us to know if we can take the suffering, the pressure, if we can still believe he loves us in the presence of great stress.

Affliction is really not what God is doing *to* us, but rather what He is doing *for* us. Those afflictions vehicularize his love, encapsulate His grace, the means by which He communicates to us something of His very presence. When that is grasped with a deep spiritual intuition, we become enveloped in peace. *Nothing* can disturb that peace, as Isaiah said (Isaiah 26:3).

Adversity is the prosperity of the great. A great person *thrives* on adversity. Abraham Lincoln became a luminary in the history of America because he thrived on adversity.

We *learn* by trials and tears. For example, would you ever learn patience if you never experienced a temptation to impatience? Would you ever practice charity, compassionate love, towards someone truly suffering if there were no suffering? If no one ever attacked you in any way or you never had an enemy, you would never practice the beautiful act of loving forgiveness? To never experience adversity is to never experience growth.

There are many purposes in suffering. Father Schaff, a Benedictine theologian, estimates that according to Scripture, there are 19 reasons for suffering. One, for instance, is patience, as stated in James 1:2-4: "Dear brothers, is your life full of difficulties, temptations and trials? Then be happy! For when the way is rough, your patience has a chance to grow. Don't try to squirm out of your problems, for when your patience is finally in full bloom, you will be ready for *anything*, strong in character, full and complete."

In Romans 5:3-5 Paul says "We should rejoice when we run into problems and trials for we know they are good for us. They help us to learn to be patient, and patience builds strength of character, helps us trust God more each time we use it until finally our hope and faith are strong and steady" — the growth process — "and when that happens we are able to hold our heads high. We know all is well for we know through all this how dearly God loves us and we feel this warm love everywhere within us because God has given us his Holy Spirit to fill our hearts with his love."

That's where Job made his mistake. He said he was a righteous man and God was allowing Satan to harass him in suffering. Certainly Job was a righteous man, but he was also a self-righteous man. That was his chief problem. Job had submission to God, but he did not have trust. What is the difference? Submission is saying I accept it, I can't fight it, I'm not going to rebel against God (Job 1:21). Trust goes beyond that and believes in God's loving providence in suffering (Job didn't reach this response until chapter 42!). In spite of (and within) that very suffering that God sends or allows to happen to me, there resides God's *love*; accepting God's love in the cross He sends us or permits to be sent to us is trust. That same God who experienced the cross in the person of Jesus says you take up your own cross now and follow Him. The trust says that there is love in that cross. Without perceiving God's love in suffering we are reduced to a "grin and bear it" response. Such faith is absolute drudgery. There is little joy or peace in that kind of suffering.

The extent to which you have peace is the extent to which you are aligned with God's will. As Dante wrote in The Divine Comedy, "In thy will, O Lord, is our peace." Only when we really rely on God as Jesus did, and trust in His will, can we have peace. It is an objectivity that comes by seeing suffering from a God's-eye-view, not the worm's-eye-view.

Once we have "put on the mind of Christ" (Philippians 2:5), we will find that the magnanimity we experience will contravene the pettiness of self-pity. Only then will we begin to experience ineffable peace in the midst of suffering.

Pray For Peace In Suffering

We need to be able to pray for peace in the midst of our sufferings and hardships. It is very easy to pray that the Lord will solve the problem, that He will heal me of this disease or this conflict with the past. George Gallup found in one of his polls that 80 percent of those who pray, pray only the prayer of petition. Very few pray the prayers of thanksgiving, praise, adoration and so on. It is seemingly very easy for us to pray for a *solution* to our problems. Very few people pray for Jesus' promise of inner peace in those problems (John 16:33) and the strength to bear those problems (II Timothy 1:8; 2:3). We tend to pray for solutions to problems, but not for predispositions needed before trying to solve the problems.

Again, Philippians 4:6-7 says to have no anxiety about *anything*. But pray about *everything*. If you do, Paul says, you will experience "the *peace* of God that passes all understanding."

Trust In God

We must build the trust that God will fulfill His promises. Victor Hugo once said that sorrow is a fruit and God does not make it grow on limbs that are too weak to bear it. How do we trust in God? The answer is in the words of Paul in II Corinthians 6:7 "We are filled with the Holy Spirit's power to help us in all this trouble." Or Romans 8:35, 39, "Who can keep Christ's love from us in calamity or trouble? Overwhelming victory is ours through Christ who loves us. Our fears, our worries ... *nothing* can separate us from the love of God." Or I Peter 5:7, "Cast your anxieties upon the Lord for he cares for you" (there Peter is quoting Psalm 55:22).

Look at Isaiah 50:7, "Because the Lord helps me, I will not be dismayed. I *know* I will triumph." Faith focusing on trust. And II Corinthians 1:10, "He helped us in our troubles and we expect him to do it again and again." Paul had tremendous faith in Christ. II Corinthians 4:9 says, "We are pursued and afflicted but God *never* abandons us." And in Psalm 50:15 the Lord says, "Trust in me in your times of trouble so I can rescue you and then you can give me glory." All of these passages imply that the trust that the Lord requires of us, especially in suffering, is a personalized form of faith. It's not the kind of faith that a widow has in the postal service as she awaits her Social Security check (non-personal faith-trust), but the kind of faith a wife has in her hardworking faithful husband to deliver his paycheck to her for the groceries each month. It's a loving trust in a faithful God to supply our needs (Philippians 3:7; 4:19).

Know The Word

We need to meditate upon the Word. Use God's love letter, the Bible, to give you the strength to deal with your problems. In Romans 15:4, Paul says, "Through the comfort of the scriptures we have hope." In Psalm 119:165 we read, "Peace have they who love your word, Lord. *Nothing* shall disturb them."

These are those who are truly head over heels in love with God's Word, deeply immersed in searching out the precious truths of the Bible (II Timothy 2:15). Anyone who devours the Word as God's love letter is never upset for long. There may be momentary upsets or disappointments but there never is any state of anxiety, fear or depression. They are not only comforted, but have great peace. Peace especially in affliction.

In II Timothy 3:17, Paul says, "His word is God's way of making us well prepared at every point, equipped for the spiritual life." There are people who call themselves

Christians who never take the Bible off the shelf except to record baptisms or weddings. There are others who pick it up rather casually once in a while. Even many who attend prayer meetings never take a Bible with them. They have never really read it, prayed about it, meditated upon it, absorbed it or allowed it to have impact on their lives, so they have little to contribute to the prayer meeting. In their personal problems those persons will be more susceptible to the buffeting effects of suffering. I've recognized this in counseling them after prayer meetings.

When I received the Baptism in the Spirit, I stayed up all night reading the Bible as if I'd never read it before *because*, as St. Thomas pointed out, those who receive the Baptism of the Spirit authentically receive the gift of understanding, one of the personal gifts listed in Isaiah 11:2. I came, by way of the gift of understanding, to see the power of God's Word for consolation, especially in suffering. All the counselors, doctors, advisors, and psychiatrists can be of great help, but their professional support has nowhere near the impact of God's Word speaking to you person-to-person.

In John 16:33, Jesus says, "These words of mine I have spoken to you in order that in me you may have peace." Peace from the Word of God in the context of suffering. "In the world," He says, "you will have many troubles and sorrows, but do not be disturbed. Cheer up, for I have overcome the world."

This is peace of mind (emotional), and it is peace of soul (spiritual) — real, everlasting peace. It comes from the Word of God. "If you abide in me, and *my word abides in you*, you may ask what you will, and it will be given you" (John 15:7).

Become Teachable

We must become docile to God, especially when he disciplines us through suffering. One of the 19 reasons for suffering given in Scripture is what we may see as punishment, but is, in fact, discipline, training. If we could learn half the lessons God wants to teach us even in the suffering of a headache, we would grow remarkably in wisdom. We come to see that in those situations of discipline we have a defect, that God is honing and polishing us.

Often we do not appreciate that fact. Once as he was spanking his little boy, a father said, "I must discipline you because you've been a naughty boy. I want you to understand that when I punish you it is because I love you." The tearful little boy replied, "I sure wish I could return your love!"

As His children, too many of us don't see love behind the disciplining hand of God. Paul learned this the hard way. In II Corinthians 12:7 he says, "I was given a physical thorn in the flesh, a messenger from Satan to hurt and bother me and to prick my pride." There is a psychological factor involved too. Paul says three different times that he begged God to make him well again and each time God said no (v. 8). But God's grace is sufficient. His power is best revealed in weakness or suffering. The lesson was learned. "Now I am glad to boast about how weak I am" (v. 9). A living demonstration of God's power. He became quite *happy* about the insults, the hardships, the persecutions, the difficulties, for the more we are weak, the more we can be made strong. The less we have, the more we learn to depend on Him. Learning to depend on God is, after all, the basic lesson of religion itself.

Paul was docile. He was *taught* by suffering. God did not answer his prayer the way Paul wanted it to be answered by removing the suffering, but by teaching him that God was receiving glory through Paul's weakness.

In I Thessalonians 5:18 we are told to thank God *in* all things. As we pointed out in the first chapter, we are not to thank God *for* all things. you don't thank God for a headache or a broken marriage, you thank Him *in* those things, because God can and will use them ultimately for our good and His glory if we love Him. Romans 8:28 plainly says, "All things work together for good to those who love him and are trying to fit into his plan ("called according to his purpose")."

In Hebrews the writer tells us not to be angry when the Lord disciplines us, neither should we be discouraged when He has to show us where we are wrong. "For when he disciplines you, it proves the Lord loves you, for whom the Lord loves, he chastises" (12:6).

"Allow God to train you. He is doing what any loving father would do for His children. Whoever heard of a child who was not corrected? If God doesn't punish you when you need it, as other fathers punish their children, then it means that you are not really God's children at all."

"Since we respect our earthly fathers even when they punish us, should we not also cheerfully submit to God's training so that we can really begin to live?" (Hebrews 12:7-10). Such submission brings with it peace.

This idea was very clear in the Old Testament in Jeremiah 30, Proberbs 3:11, Deuteronomy 8:5, Psalm 94:11 and Nehemiah 9:29. God causes some suffering to draw us into Himself.

Ask yourself these questions to see how docile you are in your suffering: Is God trying to teach me something? Am I ungenerous? Selfish? Materialistic? Rebellious? Petty? Complaining?

To answer such questions honestly takes God-given humility.

Not every case of suffering is punishment from God, as Jesus explained in the case of the blind man (John 9:3), yet punishment for sin — including ancestral sin (Exodus 20:5) — occurs more frequently than most of us are prepared to admit.

Christian maturity is not measured by the quantity or the degree of our problems, but by what we do with those problems — our response. We must learn to concentrate less on the problems — which can lead to self-pity — and more on Jesus to solve those problems. We must turn from being problem-oriented to being Christ-oriented (II Timothy 1:8; 4:5). We must turn from the problem to the problem-solver in our suffering. And that is not always as easy as it seems.

Christless suffering is like an unendorsed check. It's

worthless, a mere piece of paper. It is wasted suffering. People who seek the release, but not the teaching brought about by problems, are not learning God's lesson. They spend their entire lives in frustration. They come to absurd, untheological conclusions. "God couldn't love me," they say, "or why would He treat me this way?" Or, "God, you don't fulfill your promises. I've asked but you haven't given to me." Such an attitude means we have missed the whole point. We haven't looked into ourselves because we are too busy shaking our fists at God.

Now, to the alternatives. Either God is going to heal the situation and remove the affliction, or He will leave us with the problem and our prayer then should be for the strength to bear it. Several times in the writings of David we find him saying, "I called upon the Lord in my despair and He answered me and saved me from my affliction." Praise the Lord! We receive a gift, an answer to our prayer.

At this point we must be careful not to grab the answer to the prayer and run. People have come to prayer meetings week after week until they receive a healing of their ailment — God taking them where they are in their level of maturity. Suddenly you never see them at prayer meetings again. They grab their gift and run. No involvement in God's plan. They were only after what was in it for them, never mind God or their fellow man. Gratefully receiving the healing or solution should increase one's level of faith, and concern for others in their suffering.

Suppose God does not answer the prayer? Once you have prayed for the strength to bear it, the peace starts to take root and you get the sense of God supporting you in your affliction. Job finally sensed that after the false advice of his friends, when God spoke to him and Job acknowledged God's love had been there all along. He received an answer to prayer in that his health and wealth were restored and a new family begun. But more marvelous still was that he received a new insight, strength, peace.

Scripture is replete with victorious examples. Psalm 4:1, "You have enlarged me, Lord. You have cared for me when I was in distress"; II Corinthians 12:7, the thorn in the flesh; Philippians 3:1, "Whatever happens, be glad in the Lord"; "You do not suffer alone, you suffer with Jesus," says I Peter 4:12-13; "Be partners with Christ in his suffering."

There is now a rationale for suffering. You're walking that Calvary Road with Him, not just *watching*. In II Corinthians 1:3-4 we see another dimension — an altruistic one: "Blessed be the God and Father of our Lord Jesus Christ who comforts us in all our afflictions so that we may be able to comfort those who are in affliction with the same comforting with which we ourselves are comforted by God."

Now this peace becomes a flowing peace as Isaiah says in two places (48:18 and 66:12), flowing like a river. This peace that we have within our affliction then, once we have mastered it, begins to flow out and catch people around us. They may ask you how you could have suffered through that horrible problem and yet remain so tranquil — *and they want to experience that peace for themselves!* You begin to spread that wonderful contagion of peace and love. The Comfort given from the Lord becomes a means to comfort others around you as Paul says in II Corinthians 1:3-4.

Listen to St. Francis' magnificent definition of a cross: "The ever-lasting God has in His wisdom forseen from all eternity the cross He now presents to you as a gift from His inmost heart. This cross He now sends you He has considered with his all-knowing eyes, understood with His divine mind, tested with His wise justice, warmed with loving arms, weighed with His own hands, to see that it is not one inch too large, not one ounce too heavy, for *you*. He has blessed it with His holy name, anointed it with His grace, perfumed it with His consolation, taken one last glance at you and your courage, and then sent it to you from heaven, a special greeting from God to you, and alms of the all-merciful love of God."

That is a cross. When you understand that cross, it becomes easier to have peace in bearing that cross.

When I was conducting a retreat for some Trappist monks back in the early 1950's, an old monk came to me in the retreat master's room. I'd given a talk on suffering and he had written a poem on the topic. It was born of his years of prayer-filled suffering. I want to share it with you. As you read, make it your prayer, your deepest heart's desire, and God will grant you peace in your suffering:

Lo, there He hangs, ashened figure pinioned against the wood;
God grant that I might love Him even as I should.
I draw a little closer to feel His love divine,
And hear Him gently whisper, "Ah, precious child of mine,
If now I would embrace you, my hands would stain you red,
And if I leaned to whisper, my thorns would pierce your head."
Twas then I learned in sorrow that love demands a price;
Twas then I learned that suffering is but the kiss of Christ.

Taking a Second Look at Peace of the Cross: Heroism Made Easier

Ask Yourself (Or discuss with a study group) . . .

1. In what way does a "Lamentation prayer" help us acknowledge our problems before the Lord?

2. What spritually mature attitudes towards suffering does Paul manifest in II Corinthians 4:8-18? What do they teach us about putting problems in their proper perspective?

3. Select a problem you, or someone close to you, is experiencing. Talk about it objectively by applying Romans 8:18 and Galatians 6:9. Discuss the "worm's-eye-view" versus God's-eye-view.

4. Show how testing is essential to the believer by comparing it to the purpose of testing in technological circles.

5. How does temptation teach?

6. Explain by the life of Job how trust goes one giant step beyond mere submission. Are both submission and trust equally important?

7. Which should come first, prayer for a solution to a problem or prayer for peace in the midst of problems? Why?

8. What scriptural proof do we have that trust in God is never wasted?

9. What key role does the Bible play in developing a life of inner peace?

10. Is being docile before God a sign of weakness? What does "Docile" truly mean in our walk with Him on the road to Calvary?

11. In what way did Paul learn the lesson of docility?

12. What are some of the many purposes God has in allowing or even causing suffering?

13. How is the "contagion of peace" actually spread?

Chapter Four:

Peace Meal:
The Fruit Of The Spirit

In the megalomania department of a funny farm, there were three inmates standing around talking. One of them said, "You know, you should show me great respect. After all, I am Napoleon Bonapart."

The second said, "How could you possibly be Napoleon? *I'm* Napoleon! Who told you you were Napoleon?"

The first replied, "God told me I was Napoleon."

The third fellow, who'd been quiet all this time, said, "I did not!"

They didn't stop there. The first two turned on the third and asked "How do you know you're God?"

"It's very simple," he replied. "I decided to pray to God, to talk to Him, and when I did, I found out I was talking to myself!" This whimsical banter is a roundabout way of showing that prayer must be dialogic-interpersonal. One doesn't pray to oneself or converse with oneself in prayer. There has to be a relation between creature and Creator to have authentic prayer.

This relationship that we call prayer is very analogous to eating. When you're eating alone, you don't pass the potatoes to yourself, you simply reach for them. Eating is usually a kind of communitarian activity. Someone has said that human beings are the only animals that do not like to eat alone. That's why we have so many social events connected with meals, such as reunions, Thanksgiving and Christmas celebrations, business breakfasts, etc.

Prayer, similarly, is a togetherness and a sharing. The words of a popular hymn affirm that "God and man at table are sat down." That probably comes from Revelation 3:20, where we're reminded that Jesus stands at the door and knocks. If any man opens the door, He will come in and sup with him and he with Jesus. That doubles the emphasis that there is a communitarian, interpersonal kind of relationship in progress.

Prayer, like a meal, involves this intimate sharing., In community prayer there is a kind of "horizontal" togetherness, but in all prayer there is a "vertical" togetherness between God and us. It involves not confrontation, but conversation. Hence it is not conflictual but peaceful. It feeds on peace, that form of peace which is a fruit of the Spirit (Galatians 5:22). A really developed soul feeds on this fruit, which is an essential nutrient for a vigorous prayer life. We find, for instance, that anxieties and fears, the counterparts to peace, will certainly interfere with prayer. Fervent prayer can bring about deep peace, and conversely, peace can dispose one for fervent prayer. Prayer in some way can be both a cause and an effect of peace.

There is an ersatz peace that Jesus referred to as the peace that the world gives. It is not authentic. "The peace that I give you," Jesus said (John 14:27), "is not the fragile peace that the world gives to you." In guruism and other forms of Eastern religion, there is a seeking of self-fulfillment, an inwardness, characterized by a form of peace that comes with tranquil meditation. Such egocentric peace, produced by mental gymnastics, provides a feeling of self-fulfillment, a peace with one's self. In and of itself it is not authentic peace because in it I am "passing the potatoes" to myself. It is totally different from that peace related to God which engages us in a shared "peace meal," an interchange of deep, serene love. This is what Jesus refers to as "*my* peace."

When Jesus speaks of supping with an individual and the individual with Him, there are two implications of a prayer relationship, a close intimacy of communing. First, He does not say if you open the door He will call you out. He says if you open the door, *He will come in*. He is speaking of something very interior, very intimate — God, in fact, coming into us. Secondly, it is an interfacing — something mutual: "I will sup with him and he will sup with me." When we have experienced this mutuality, this close intertwining of creature and Creator, we will have understood the wide difference between Christic peace and the peace that the world gives. "Abide in me and I in you," like the vine and branches, is the requirement for the bearing of fruit (John 15:5), including that fruit of the Spirit called peace.

Eastern meditation is a prayerless form of meditation. While it could *predispose* someone for real prayer, in and of itself it is not genuine prayer. Norms for genuine prayer can be found in the oft-quoted twenty-third psalm: ("You prepare a table for me"); (note the peace images: "beside still waters,"etc.). Psalm 34 invites us to "*taste* and see that the *Lord is good*" — not just to taste the feeling of self-contained serenity. Our peace meal with the Lord is a "tasting" in a relaxed sharing of an interpersonal experience in an atmosphere of mutual *love* (you don't eat with your enemies or even strangers). At this "prayer banquet" we can hear the Lord say to please pass the trust. We ask Him to please pass the peace. We give the Lord loving trust and He responds with His love-filled peace. "They will have peace whose mind is stayed *upon the Lord*" (Isaiah 26:3), not on ourselves in confining self-isolation, as non-Christian Eastern methods propose.

Crudens lists nine different meanings of the word peace as it is found in Scripture. We will deal with it here only as it relates to prayer. Peace may be said to be the root of prayer and the fruit of prayer, just as the chicken gives rise to the egg as well as the egg giving rise to the chicken.

Keep in mind that there are forms of peace, both natural and supernatural, unrelated to prayer. Jesus referred to a natural peace — even to the lashing waves He commanded, "Peace — be still!" But the natural peace of human anxiety allayed was not beyond His purview. In forgiving the adulterous woman (Luke 7:50), He spoke of a spiritual, supernatural peace: "Go in peace. Your sins are forgiven." Yet, in the next chapter of Luke He says the same words — "go in peace" — but this time He is not speaking to a woman who was forgiven but to a woman who was healed. In the first case, a woman was healed of sin, a spiritual leprosy, and in the second, a woman was healed of a physical infirmity. He was using the word peace in different ways in each case: In the first, go in peace, you no longer are in conflict with God — freedom from evil; in the second, go in peace, you no longer have to worry about your sickness — freedom from anxiety. Two different forms of peace (supernatural and natural) and yet expressed in the same words.

Within the category of the supernatural there are, again, two kinds of peace: the peace *with* God and the peace *of* God. The Scripture makes clear distinctions between those two categories of supernatural peace. Peace *with* God is the immediate predisposition for the peace *of* God. Your prayer life can be facilitated by understanding the difference between the two. Peace *with* God is the fruit of *metanoia*, the Greek word used in theology to mean turning from sin to God — that is, the total giving of oneself to God and receiving His mercy and forgiveness. Metanoia is the radical experience that is often called "getting saved" or being "born again." That results in peace *with* God as stated in Romans 5:1, and expatiated in verse 10. A sinner is at enmity with God; the very moment that he repudiates his sin by repentance, he receives the mercy of God. He is reconciled with God — *"at peace"* with God.

The degree of this peace with God depends upon the depth of that commitment of "living by faith in the Son of God" who has loved *me* and delivered himself for *me* (Galatians 2:20) (Notice the person-to-person commitment). The immediate effect of that recognition of God's presence and that personal committed relationship ("salvation" in the initial sense of the word), is peace *with* God. If it is genuinely deep, the person experiences an incredible sense of peace and security, knowing that "those the Father has given me, no one can snatch from my hand" (John 10:28-29). They know they are free from sin, because "when the Son of God makes you free, you are free indeed" (John 8:36). That's the true fruit of *metanoia* — a freedom from sin that puts one at peace *with* God.

The peace *of* God on the other hand, is the fruit of the Holy Spirit (Romans 14:17). Galatians 5:22 speaks of the fruit of the Spirit which is love. But that fruit, like an orange, has segments: joy, *peace*, patience, kindness, goodness, gentleness, faithfulness, self-control. Peace is thus one segment of this fruit of the Spirit.

As you move beyond the peace *with* God to the peace *of* God, you begin to realize something is happening to your interior life. You experience an atmosphere of loving companionship in security; the Lord begins to reveal Himself in deeper dimensions. The peace *with* God is the fruit of God's *forgiving love* that removes guilt. The peace *of* God is the fruit of God's *unitive love* (John 16:33: "united to me, you have peace") and it removes hostility (resentment) and anxiety.

Together, these two forms of peace are antidotes for the three major syndromes of a neurotic personality; namely, hostility, guilt and anxiety. The Scripture tells us in 13 places how to dispose of both the guilt and hostility through receiving and giving forgiveness. When those two syndromes are gone, the third one, anxiety, will dissolve by itself. This allows peace to flourish since, expressed negatively, peace is the absence of anxiety. Permeated with God's unitive love, it becomes supernatural "peace of heart" (also called "peace of soul").

Thus peace *with* God results from *turning to God*, while the peace *of* God is a result of *abiding in God*.

The "peace of mind", that is, the peace of one's conscience, is the effect of the peace *with* God, whereas the "peace of heart" or "peace of soul" that Jesus so often spoke about is the effect of the peace *of* God.

Peace *with* God is spoken of in a number of Scriptures. Romans 5:1 says, "You have peace with God because of what Christ has done." There we see the relationship between *redemption* and the effect of receiving it, or *salvation*. In Acts 10:36 we find Peter speaking to Cornelius: "You have peace with God through Jesus." In Luke 2:14 we find the angels singing of peace on earth to men of goodwill. Some commentators say that is "men of God's will," men who have related themselves to God's will ("on earth as it is in heaven"). In Ephesians 2:17, Paul speaks about the good news of peace reconciling the Jews to the Gentiles because both have been reconciled to Christ (the *metanoia* or salvation concept again).

The peace *of* God is most clearly highlighted by Jesus in John 14:27: "*My* peace I give you, not as the world gives to you . . . Let not your hearts be troubled, neither let them be afraid." Again, prophecying tribulations, He assured His disciples: "In me (united to me) you will have peace" (John 16:33). His first words to them that first Easter evening, as they hid in fear, were: "Peace be to you;" He even repeated that phrase for emphasis (John 20:19.21), and again at his next appearance (John 20:26).

The peace of God as a concept is further analyzed in the epistles. Peter prays that the Dispersion exiles experience an increasing sense of God's peace (I Peter 1:2), implying that progress is possible in this fruit of the Spirit (general spiritual progress is scenarioed in II Peter 1). The Christocentric dimension of the peace of God is emphasized by Paul in Colossians 3:15, showing that peace of God has to be interpersonal, Christ-related.

In Philippians 4:6-7, the most remarkable passage to deal with peace, Paul calls it the peace that passes all understanding. "Don't worry about *anything*. Instead pray about *everything* in supplication and thanksgiving. *If* you do this (conditional), you will experience peace of God which is more wonderful than the human mind can understand. His peace will keep your thoughts and your heart quiet and at rest *as you trust Christ Jesus*." There's that intimate relationship again. The peace meal is now a communion situation where you are communing, relating, trusting.

There are degrees in this relationship. As you move towards the more ethereal dimensions of that kind of trust-spawned peace, you will find yourself not in prayer of meditation, not even in affective prayer, but rapidly moving into acquired contemplation and beyond, into infused contemplation, the higher octane forms of prayer.

Scripture relates peace to prayer. In Matthew 11:27-30 Jesus says the Father is known only by the Son and by those to whom the Son reveals Him. "Now come to me (the unitive aspect of the peace of God) all you who labor and are heavy laden (anxieties, fears, burdens), and I will give you rest (peace)." You're not going to receive peace standing over there. You must come to Him. Don't seek this kind of peace in transcendental meditation or Eastern mantras, but only in union with Jesus.

He goes on to say, "Learn of me (a growth process of learning in a school of peace) for I am meek (not full of anger, but at peace with myself) and humble of heart (no pompous pride, no anxious struggling to get to the top of the ladder of success), and you shall find rest (peace) for your soul." He's talking about revealing Himself, revealing the Father (God's side of the prayer dialogue) and our response (coming to Him), and then He will give us peace (to demonstrate that we have truly encountered Him in a meaningful way). That double passage is a kind of study of the relationship between peace and prayer.

We find a hint of it in Proverbs 14:26, "Reverence (prayer attitude) for the Lord brings security and peace." One of the most quoted passages, of course, is Isaiah 26:3, "He shall keep in perfect peace him whose thoughts are stayed upon the Lord (whose thoughts turn often to the Lord) for he trusts in the Lord."

Have you ever noticed that the lack of interior peace

that we generally refer to as anxiety is experienced by those whose lives are problem-oriented? They spend a great deal of their thinking life focused on problems (The Latin origin of the word "anxiety" means to choke). Benzel once said that anxiety and prayer are like fire and water. You cannot be focused on your problem if you are fully in prayer because your focus is then on Jesus. Real prayer is *God*-focus as opposed to *problem*-focus. *Peace* as opposed to *anxiety* or non-peace. You simply cannot be focused on anxiety when you're focused on the Lord. Remember the wonderful old hymn that says, "Turn your eyes upon Jesus, look full in His wonderful face. The things of earth will grow strangely dim in the light of His glory and grace."

Try this experiment. If you feel anxious, perhaps from the pressures of freeway traffic or some other stress or pressure, try praising God. I am often in a hurry to get somewhere and find myself being slowed by heavy traffic. At these times I often sing in tongues, praising God in prayer,. Suddenly, the stress simply evaporates. By the time I arrive at my destination, I feel very tranquil. "Come unto me . . . and I will give you rest."

Don't discount the possibility that anxiety can be caused by a spirit of anxiety that delights in distrubing one's peace. Such demonic spirits are very prevalent in this age of anxiety. There are evil influences that range from the spirit of adultery to divorce, confusion to faithlessness, and human infirmities of many kinds. One of the most highly operative is the evil spirit of anxiety. Satan particularly sends that one out to attack persons who are seriously trying to become holy. He knows that if he can create an anxiety state in an individual, that person's prayer will suffer. He would never simply try to convince someone that prayer is bad, because no one would buy that suggestion or temptation. What he does instead is fill them with anxiety and thereby focus their attention on the conflicts around them rather than on God. These are the very persons who ask why God never answers their prayers. The question ought to be, why don't they ever *really* pray? When they attempt to pray, it becomes a problem-centered prayer. By contrast, a God-centered prayer glorifies Him, praises Him, worships Him.

There is nothing wrong with a prayer of petition that seeks a solution to a problem. You can't get away from the problematic when dealing with petitionary prayer. But, when there is an *anxiety in that prayer* which Paul forbids in Philippians 4:6, then it is not really a good prayer of petition. It is simply childish whining, rather than a seeking after God's will. It is all, "I want, I want . . ." and never "Thy will be done," or a sincere "Hallowed by Thy Name." It is not God-centeredness, it's self-centeredness. Until we can learn to use petitionary prayer in a way in which we seek not the consolation of God, but the God of consolation, we will never move into a higher level of prayer life; we will hit a plateau in our ascent toward higher levels of peace.

Worry and prayer are at spiritual odds. "Don't worry about anything but pray about everything," Paul says. Are you worried about anything at all? Health, family, marriage, drug addiction, your children straying from the church? If you are really worried, you are violating a command of Jesus; six times in Luke 12 and Matthew 6 He commands us not to worry. He says not to worry about food, drink, clothes, *things*. "Why be like the heathen who take pride in all these things? Your heavenly Father already knows perfectly well you have need of these things, and He will give them to you if you seek first the kingdom of God and his holiness. All these other things will be taken care of."

Worry places you out of the will of God. And to the extent that you are worried, you are placing roadblocks in the path of prayer. You cannot get close to God when you are worried because you are focused on material things, or dwelling on the problems instead of on the God who holds the solutions to those problems. Peter, while walking on the water, took his eyes off Jesus and looked anxiously at the waves around him. It was only then that he began to sink (Matthew 14:30). Look not to the problems but to the problem-solver.

In Colossians 3:15, Paul speaks of the peace of heart that comes from Christ. If you have repented and have committed yourself to Christ in a deeply personal way, then you experience peace with God. If not, then you have been perhaps only sacramentalized, but not evangelized; you have been baptized, but it is not a "completed" baptism. Unfortunately, most Christians have not really been evangelized. They have heard the Gospel message, but have never committed themselves in a personal way to a one-to-one relationship with God, as Pope John Paul II lamented. Most Christians then don't have an *experienced* peace with God, which even has psychologocal benefits, and even some psychosomatic benefits.

Still fewer Christians experience peace *of* God. It is not simply freedom from guilt, not just the tremendous joy of knowing you have one foot in heaven. It goes beyond that to a peace that is an utterly ineffable tranquility — a Spirit-given foretaste, in some way, of the very peace of heaven.

If you don't have that, you have a major roadblock to your spiritual development. If your prayer life, your "peace meal" with Jesus, cannot be enjoyed, then you are suffering spiritual indigestion. You have not learned to enjoy the fruit of the Spirit that is real peace.

That classical passage of Philippians 4:6-7 entails three main thrusts about peace. First, it is transcendent, because Paul says that this peace "surpasses all understanding"; secondly, it is protective because it will "*keep* your hearts and minds in Christ Jesus"; and thirdly, it will be continuous, an ongoing protection ("*will* keep").

Let us look at these three main emphases separately. First, the peace that passes understanding is one that you cannot possibly verbalize or explain. It is an incredible experience quite unlike any other. When some people have gone into a coma and are technically, clinically, dead, many of them have a recall of a "life after life" experience (OBE or "out-of-body" experience). Upon being revived, they glowingly report that the experience was so *peaceful*, that they had no desire to return to this life, that it angered them to have to come back. They say it is an essentially indescribable experience. They are unable to give many details because there is nothing in our human experience that compares with it. They are literally at a loss for words.

Such is a mere hint of the peace of God experienced in heaven. It remotely compares with what Paul talks about in Philippians. In even the limited way it is experienced in deep contemplative prayer on earth, it is difficult to describe in words. This level of peace characterizes a deep prayer stance — a fusion with God in profound communion, which in mystical theology is referred to as an "apotheosis."

When it surpasses human understanding, it means this peace is beyond human ability to create. There is no way anyone could ever crank up the peace *of* God. But peace *with* God can be induced by an act of repentance with acceptance of and dedication to the Lord. Peace *with* God comes through human action; the peace *of* God is a gift of celestial serenity, scooped out by the Spirit from God's own ocean of divine tranquility.

The peace of God can't come through transcendental meditation or yoga which are forms of temporary, humanly contrived peace. There are countless human techniques for creating temporary peace through various forms of mental gymnastics (mantras, self-hypnosis, eye-focusing, etc.). God's peace, however, surpasses natural peace in a supernatural communion unobtainable by man's efforts.

Do you desire peace? How much control do you have over worry? Will worry — nonpeace — add a single moment to your life? (Matthew 6:29). When you *know* that God is in control, you can easily launch out in total reliance on Him. He will "keep you in perfect peace if your mind is stayed on him," as Isaiah says.

Secondly, this peace of God is protective, *keeping* our hearts and minds in Jesus. In the original Greek, the word is associated with the function of a garrison or guarding shield. This peace will build a wall of protection around you, so that *nothing* can disturb you. Your mind and your thinking processes will not be disturbed and your affections, your heart, will also be at peace. There will be no conflict in the drives of your personality.

Now this brings up two questions. What does the peace of God protect and what does it protect from? "Heart and mind" mean it protects the emotions, the affections, the purposes (goals and intents), our thoughts, our volition (willing act) and grants freedom from anxiety in bringing to effect our decisions.

In what way can our emotions be protected? Of the 27 emotions, anxiety is the most corrosive in its effects on the human personality, after guilt. With the peace of God, you have a freedom of emotional life where you can rejoice as Jesus did. The same Jesus that said, "My peace I give you" also said "I give you my joy that your joy may be full" (John 15:11). Peace and joy are wed in Christ's love. His emotions were well integrated. The affections are orderly in the interior man that is being protected, or garrisoned, in this peace of God.

A man who desires more pay must first ask himself, "*Why* do I want more pay?" To be a better provider for the family, for prestige, for increased materialism? This peace of God when present, settles that conflict; there is no anxiety because an order has entered into his motivation. "Seek *first* the kingdom of God," then there will be order. This reflects St. Augustine's classical definition of peace as "tranquility that results from order."

All forms of peace have this common denominator, and that is tranquility that results from proper order. The ultimate peace is found in love of God, the highest order. Putting it in a psychological framework, the *ordered* personality has the emotions, the affections, the thoughts, the volitions all in order. That person is very well disposed for prayer. There is no clutter in the mind of that individual, who hence possesses a tranquility, a serenity by which one is disposed for optimum prayer.

At this point, prayer is no longer a burden. It becomes an enjoyable experience. One eagerly looks forward to the time to be free of any kind of material distractions and be alone with the Lord.

Such peace protects from care, anxiety, inner sufferings and conflicts. It will "keep our hearts and minds in Christ Jesus." Everything else is outside the garrison walls. The nagging doubts and anxieties that prevent us from "clean" prayer will dissipate.

Thirdly, this is perpetual peace. In the Greek, the proper meaning is: "He will keep on keeping you at peace in Christ Jesus." The King James version in Isaiah phrases the concept beautifully: "Thou will *keep* him in perfect peace whose mind is *stayed* on Thee" (Isaiah 26:3). Present your needs to the Lord and stop perpetually worrying and you will have perpetual peace instead. "I will never, never forsake you, says the Lord" (Hebrews 13:5). He has made a perpetual promise. Knowing God is never going to let you down, you can simply relax confidently in His loving arms.

So be at peace, and let your heart *grow* in peace as Peter says. Then you will have, in your daily prayer experience, a kind of peace which is but a foretaste of the "peace meal" we shall enjoy in the banquet of heaven. It not only comes from, but will draw us deeper into, the very heart of God.

Taking a Second Look
at Peace Meal:
The Fruit Of The Spirit

Ask Yourself (Or discuss with a study group) . . .

1. In what way is peace both a cause and effect?

2. What kind of peace does the world give, and what makes it so fragile?

3. What are the essential differences between peace *with* God and the peace *of* God?

4. What two forms of peace are expressed in Jesus' words "go in peace"?

5. What does I Peter 1:2 imply about progress in the spiritual life?

6. Why don't prayer and anxiety mix?

7. What three aspects of peace are contained in Philippians 4:6-7?

8. How is the concept of garrisoning crucial to the peace of God?

9. How does an "ordered" Christianity result when peace is claimed and practiced as specified in Philippians 4:6-7?

10. How does the perpetual promise of Hebrews 13:5 square with the peace of God?

Chapter Five:

Interior Peace:
The Universal Quest
For Christ

There was a man who went to the doctor with a serious sore throat and cough. The doctor examined him and asked if he had seen any other doctor about the problem.

"No, but I did consult the pharmacist at the drug store," replied the man hoarsely.

Whereupon the doctor sarcastically asked, "And what kind of stupid advice did he give you?"

The man looked the doctor in the eye and said, "He told me to come and see you."

We are open to a great deal of wrong advice. Paul warns us that we must be careful not to be turned one way and another by the confused and confusing advice. Make certain, he says, that it is truly from the Lord, the great physician.

"We shouldn't be like children forever changing our minds because someone has told us or cleverly lied to us. Instead we should lovingly follow the truth at all times speaking truly, dealing truly, living truly and so become more and more in every way like Christ, the head of the church. Under his direction, the whole body fits together perfectly" (Ephesians 4:14).

Our real consultant and guide, our mentor, is Jesus.

He is the One through whom we go to the Father. He is the one through whom the Father communicates Himself to us because He is the Word, the articulation of the God-presence with us and within us.

There is a universal quest for peace, freedom from fear and potential harm. It is built into our very nature to seek security, a powerful and universal drive, even in the hierarchy of values in our materialistic society. A Gallup Poll found that 40 percent of Americans rank a desire for peace of mind above money, wealth, health, happy relationships or anything you can name. The rest, too, placed it very high on the list.

Some philosopher has said the pursuit of peace is universal, but the *kind* of peace one pursues is a measure of the moral state of a person and the system of values that person possesses. If you want to discover how sublime a person's ideals are, how one actually comes to terms with life, ask this one question: "What kind of peace are you seeking?"

The answer may be peace of an international or interracial kind, peace between labor and management, peace of heart, mind or soul — perhaps even peace with God. Peace comes in many forms but ultimately what people want is interior peace, the peace *of* God, even when they don't know what it is, or don't know how to articulate that desire.

Negatively, we often think of peace as the opposite of war. More positively, let us take another look at the classical 4th century definition from St. Augustine: "tranquility which results from proper order." When everything is properly ordered, we have peace. The highest faculty is the will, the highest operation of which is to love. Love has many objects, the highest of which is infinite good — God. Hence, the most perfect human act is that of the will when it loves God. When one's entire being is focused on God ("Thou shalt love the Lord thy God with all thy whole heart, mind, soul and all they strength . . ."), then you have order. All beneath the highest is subordinated (ordered) to the highest. The resultant tranquility we call peace.

That is why peace follows love as a fruit of the Spirit in Galations 5:22. Anyone who is truly a master of the great art of love is at peace. If you love God, your fellow man, and have a proper self-love which is God-centered, then you have mastered love and true peace naturally follows.

Because of that basic common denominator of peace, we can determine the value system of a person based on the kind of peace they seek.

Most of us grasp at straws, thirsting for peace while implicitly denying God's promise that it is within our grasp. It is as near as our Bible, God's revelation. We are surrounded with the fresh water of His presence and still we do not drink, because we think all there is is saltwater. Peace is not unreachable. Not only is it there for the drinking, but He will dip down and hand it to us. "My peace I *give* you" (John 14:27).

We stumble about experimenting, drinking the bilge water instead of going to the real source of peace. Throughout the history of mankind we find people frenetically searching for this peace, and many end up spiritually bankrupt. Seneca, a Roman philosopher of the Stoic persuasion, was a contemporary of St. Paul's. He wrote words about peace that were almost identical to Christ's: "Not as the world gives unto you will I give you the secret of peace." Yet this man was a pagan philosopher, so his explanation of how to acquire peace was totally different from Christ's. Seneca said we come by peace through apathy, dismissing our feelings and desires. We must never allow ourselves joy or sorrow; rather we must be stoical. One who is genuinely apathetic, claimed Seneca, will never experience true disappointment nor be disturbed in any way.

That's a little like the man who took his car into a garage and told the repairman that his horn was apathetic. "What do you mean your horn is apathetic?" asked the mechanic. "Well," replied the customer, "it just doesn't give a hoot!"

People who are apathetic have a bad kind of indifference. *Holy* indifference is accepting God's will, placing no demands upon Him. *Unholy* indifference means you don't care whether you attend church, read the Bible, acquire virtues or work out your marriage differences or not. That kind of indifference is both sinful and sick. The Stoics were advocating apathy. But to anesthetize all your desires is to drink the bilge water of life, when fresh water is available.

Caesar wrote, shortly after Seneca's time, of his struggles to obtain peace through self-sufficiency. He found it did not work. In our modern day, we have something close to that — not so much apathy as egotistic self-sufficiency, or secular humanism. It holds the position that, because we have great scientists, doctors and technologists, we don't need religion or God for anything. All we need do is use our human ingenuity. God is dead, God is sleeping, God is silent. Secular humanism is the vestibule of atheism.

Jesus does not accept that seeking peace through self-sufficiency. It is not His kind of peace.

When we follow these philosophers and their substitutes for religion, we embark on a path of absolute misery. In Colossians 2:8-10 Paul warns, "Don't let others spoil your faith and joy with their philosophies, their wrong and shallow answers built on human thought and ideas instead of on what Christ has said. In Christ, there is all of God *and* man. When you have Christ, you have *everything* and you are filled with God through your union with Christ. He is the highest ruler with authority over every other power." You don't have to turn to false philosophies in your quest for all these things that Christianity genuinely offers.

Yet people are deluded in droves. Proverbs 16:25 says, "Before every man there lies a wide and pleasant road he thinks is right but it often ends in death."

Once a former prostitute who had been shot by her best friend was being interviewed on television's 700 Club. She was paralyzed and confined to a wheelchair. She told how she had forgiven the girl who had shot her and had even attempted to have the girl's 15-year sentence shortened. She told, too, how she had had to earn $300 a day to support her pimps and her drug habit before accepting Christ and becoming reborn. Her search for peace was through heroin addiction. And that, though an extreme example, is so typical of our society. She, thank God, came to realize she had been looking in all the wrong places. She finally found the answer in Jesus.

There is no true peace in stoicism, apathy, humanism. Buddhism promises peace if you rid yourself of all desire, the root cause of all disappointment. This then leads to the destruction of personality, consciousness of yourself, and eventually to nirvana. Nirvana is absence of all conflict, a kind of soul death. It certainly is not a life. Eastern religions are all built on self-fulfillment, never union with God. They seek answers from within, but not from the God within.

At first blush it seems that St. Paul affirms the Buddhist philosophy. He says in Colossians 3:5 to rid overselves of sinful, earthly desires. "Away, then, with sinful earthly things. Deaden the evil desires lurking within you. Have nothing to do with sexual sin, impurity, lust. Don't worship the good things of life for that is a form of idolatry." It is a good thing to deaden your unruly desires, but it is a negative thing that in no way leads to love *by itself*. Without Paul's other remarks about growing in union with God through Christ, this advice of his would be, by itself, paganistic.

I was driving in West Los Angeles one day. Usually I am so careful never to pick up hitchhikers, as FBI statistics tell us that three out of five hitchhikers have a police record. But this day I picked up a young man, and we were soon talking about religion. He was attending the Universal Church Triumphant, a cult religion that took over a seminary where I once taught. As he was so enthusiastic about it, I questioned him as to what he was gaining. Before I dropped him off, we talked of peace.

"You know," he said, "I had what I thought was peace before I got into this car. They told me there was nothing that could ever disturb that peace but you've made me rethink this whole thing."

The hunger was there. He wanted God and the answers to life. He needed to know how to cope with this life's problems and fears. Is it a string of meaningless anxieties? He was earnestly searching and I was able to jolt him a little further along the path in his search.

Transcendental Meditation, Hinduism and other forms of Eastern religion involve various forms of idol worship. When repeating any of the 16 mantras supposed to create a mellow mental state, a person is in fact invoking one of the names of a false god in the Shankhara tradition of Hinduism. The leaders who guide others in these religions experience eight times the national suicide rate. Peace? You have to experience a great deal of anxiety or depression to be tempted to suicide; thus the peace that they offer cannot be a lasting peace. It is not a good and desireable peace, but a false and empty one. Christ's peace is everlasting.

Many people never learn the difference between the false peace of the world and the real peace that Jesus gives.

What is Jesus' peace? First of all, it is not as the world gives (John 14:27); it is supernal. Paul follows that up in Philippians 4:7 saying that it is a peace that surpasses all human understanding, all human contrivance. It cannot be structured nor engineered because it is God's gift.

In Isaiah 26:3 that peace is called *perfect* peace. Notice the *giver* of that perfect peace, Isaiah says, is the Lord. It is a relationship between creature and Creator. The perfect peace comes to the one whose mind remains on the Lord "because he *trusts* the Lord," an act of faith-love that brings that peace about. "His mind is stayed on the Lord," that is, he maintains a habit of prayer. St. Cyprian said the chalice of the soul will carry as much peace as the size of the chalice. The deeper our prayer union with God, the deeper our chalice and the more peace God pours into it.

Secondly, Jesus' peace is universal. It is offered to all and obtainable by all, not just for the philosophic few. "If *anyone* thirst, let him come unto me."

Jesus' peace has a *power*, a characteristic of charismatic peace. As a fruit of the Spirit (Galatians 5:22), it carries a charismatic dimension. Luke 24:49 and Acts 1:8 tell us, "When the Spirit comes upon you, you will receive *power* . . . " Romans 8:2, II Peter 1:3 and many other passages speak of that same power.

It is the power that is in the peace of Christ. It has the power to lift you above temptation. Not that you are going to be free of all temptations, but you will have power to deal with the temptations, the power to shield yourself from the anxieties and uncertainties of life now and in the future. You will still experience troubles and difficulties. Romans 8:23 says, "Even we who have the Spirit also groan within us. We, too, anticipate that day when God will give us *full* rights as his children, including new bodies." But this power will enable us in some way to transcend temptations and suffering. In Hebrews 13:20, the author says, "May the God of peace equip you with all you need to do his will." He will empower you! But notice, it is the "God of *peace*" who equips you.

We see this combination of power and peace in Mark 4:39 where Jesus calmed the sea with the words, "Peace, be still." A perfect, extraordinary calm came over that lake. The Sea of Galilee is an unusual place where a storm can blow up within minutes. Who was this that the winds and sea should obey Him, His disciples wondered aloud. What power there was behind that peace!

Peter lost his peace when walking upon the water. In losing his peace and tranquility by taking his eyes off Jesus, he gave into anxiety, as the waves raged around him; he lost the corresponding charismatic, miracle-working power — and began to sink. (Matthew 14:30).

There is such a contrast between Christ's power-laden optimistic, everlasting peace and the pessimistic, temporary peace of the world! Buddhism is but one example of the latter. Its literature is full of a kind of scornful wailing about the vanity and futility of the world. Buddhism doesn't present a Heavenly Father who is going to face the sorrow with you, with His arm around your shoulders. The essential elements of love and the divine are missing. No warmth, nothing to temper the world's anguish. True peace must be not only intra-personal, but also inter-personal — resulting from the interfacing of creature with Creator.

From the Christian point of view, peace comes after surrender to God's love and to the will of God expressed in love, including the providential love that is camou-flaged in suffering. To make sense of the hardships, we must surrender to God's love and allow God to grant us His peace in the midst of hardship. We find Jesus re-minding us that we will experience troubles. John 16:33 says, "I told you all this so you will have peace of heart and mind. Here on earth you will have many trials and sorrows. But cheer up, for I have overcome the world." In John 14:27 Jesus says, "I am leaving you with the gift of peace of mind and heart, the peace that is not fragile like the world gives. Don't be troubled or afraid." Isn't this a paradox? Jesus said we would have troubles, but not be troubled!

He says He is not going to exempt us from problems until we reach heaven. But He promised strength to bear the problems. Thus, this power in peace is clearly *person*-oriented. "Come unto *me*." Jesus said. "*I* will refresh you and give you rest for your soul." Don't go through all the wasted philosophic motions, but come unto the Person of Jesus Christ.

Jesus is the magnet that attracts us. Once we've understood that, our lives must become Jesus-oriented. St. Paul was a master at this — centering his entire life on Christ. He recognized that Christ had won the victory for us. Why do we persist in futile struggle, in swimming against the stream of life. when we could be relaxing in the arms of Christ?

In John 14:1 Jesus tells us, "You have trusted in God, now trust me." All through the gospel of John, Jesus says to focus on Him and we will have peace. Colossians 3:15 reminds us that that peace comes from Christ.

In Psalm 34:19 we read, "God is close to those whose

hearts are breaking. He rescues those who are humbly sorry for their sins. The good man does not escape all troubles." Some of the greatest saints and martyrs had troubles and were persecuted. Paul was a good man but he was nonetheless shipwrecked and scourged and starved half to death. "But the Lord helps him in each and every problem," the psalmist continues.

Psalm 50:15 says, "I don't need your sacrifices of flesh and blood. What I want from you is your true thanks. I want you to trust me in your time of trouble so that I can rescue you and you can give me glory." This Christic peace is realistic in the sense that it says you're not going to be free of trouble. Romans 8:23 indicates that even the plants and animals suffer.

It is not material things of the world that bring peace. Some people hunger for freedom from poverty. "If I only had money," they say, "I wouldn't have to worry." King David and King Solomon might beg to differ. They had fabulous wealth, yet experienced personal disasters of great magnitude. In King Solomon's case, the amassing of great wealth and a thousand wives for political leverage and show led to a lack of humility and to idol worship that eventually destroyed him. The richer you become, the more obligations you acquire. "Noblesse oblige," as the pithy French expression has it.

I like the words of the book of Proberbs that say, "Lord, may I never be really poor and may I never be really rich." Extreme poverty, of course, is misery. You don't desire that, and God doesn't want you to be impoverished either. But extreme wealth is often a tragedy — when it leads to *love* of money. According to I Timothy 6:10, the *love* of money is the root of *all* evil. When you cannot stop grabbing for the "good" things of life, you are trapped. Beyond a certain point, you not only do not gain peace from your wealth, it begins to disturb what peace you do have, especially if you are not giving to the poor from your income. II Corinthians 9:5-7 and Luke 12:48 tell us God will give us much in order that we may give away much. Two blessings occur. "Those in need are helped *and* they overflow in thanksgiving to God."

Paul says, "There will not only be enough for your own needs, but plenty left over to give joyfully to others." The Bible says the godly man gives to the poor and his good deeds will be an honor to him forever.

God wants you to have wealth in order to spend it. The more you spend and give to the poor, the more you will get back. Many scriptures speak of this. One of my favorite paraphrased psalms: "When you help the poor, you are lending to the Lord and he pays wonderful interest on your loan" (Psalm 19:17).

To be sure, you gain a certain amount of peace from having enough money to pay your bills and not having to worry where your next meal is coming from. God wants you to have financial security. *But*, if your entire being is focused on that as an ultimate goal to satisfy the immortal dimension of your personhood, then you are a materialist and on the wrong track. Instead of material things serving us as God says they should ("Be *in* the world, not *of* the world"), the things themselves become false gods. I John 2:15 speaks of various ways in which we can practice idolatry through worldliness: "Stop loving this evil world and what it offers you for when you love these things, you show that you do not really love God, for all these worldly things such as craze for sex, ambition to buy everything that appeals to you, the pride that comes from wealth and the importance placed on fame and reputation, are not from God. They are from the evil world itself. This world is fading away and these evil, forbidden things will go with it, but whoever keeps doing the will of God will live forever."

James 1:27 says, "Don't be soiled and dirtied by your contacts with the world." Certainly you must have contacts with the world, but don't allow them to captivate you! Don't become so fascinated with money that you just live for that horse race or that stock market windfall (In that context, you might meditate on II Corinthians 6, Colossians 3:5 and Romans 13:13).

Jesus prayed for His apostles at the Last Supper as recorded in John 16; "Heavenly Father, I pray not that you take them out of the world, but leave them uncontaminated by the world." Worldly things are not intrinsically evil, but neither are they the absolutes.

St. Augustine tried every sin he could discover, and when he couldn't think of any new sins to commit, he explored a moral theology book for others. His mother, St. Monica, prayed for him all those years and the Lord captured him. His mother was named a saint because she converted her son through prayer.

Anti-worldliness is summarized by St. Augustine in chapter one, book one of his classic confessions: "Our hearts are made for thee, O Lord, and they cannot find rest (peace) until they rest in thee."

Taking a Second Look
at Interior Peace:
The Universal Quest For Christ

Ask Yourself (Or discuss with a study group) . . .

1. How is it possible to determine a person's value system based on the kind of peace that is sought?

2. What is the essential difference between holy and unholy indifference?

3. Why are purely human philosophies so empty and incapable of bringing true peace?

4. What is it about Eastern religions that is so opposed to God's way?

5. Define Jesus' peace.

6. What is the power contained in the peace of Christ? What does it enable a Christian to do?

7. In what way is God's love camouflaged in suffering?

8. How do the sufferings of St. Paul demonstrate God's love and power in his life?

9. When can and when can't material possessions bring peace?

Chapter Six:

Christ's Comfort: Making Peace With Stress

There was a tenant in an apartment house who was complaining to the landlord about the people upstairs.

"Last night," he said, "they were stomping on the floor and deliberately making noise until two o'clock in the morning!"

"Did they keep you awake?" the landlord asked.

"Oh, no," replied the tenant. "Fortunately, I happened to be practicing my tuba at the time."

People cause people stress. We hardly realize the stress we generate for others, being rather much more conscious of the stress others cause us. Stress is not something we can escape. Periodicals often carry stories about the latest findings on stress. America ranks as the leading nation in sheer numbers of pill-poppers in the world, with most of the top 10 prescription drugs sold in this country prescribed to fight stress or stress-related illnesses (Valium and the like). We try to deal with stress chemically through nicotine, alcohol, marijuana and cocaine. Of course, those things do not actually reduce stress. They may reduce some of the symptoms temporarily, but ultimately they increase the stress, especially when addiction causes stress in anticipation of the next "fix." The chemical approach to stress contains no satisfactory answers nor lasting relief.

Some interesting studies have emerged from what has been called "the age of anxiety." Dr. Herbert Spiegel, one of the world's foremost experts on stress, has proven that there is no way to prevent the body from being affected by stress. There is always a psychosomatic response. It will usually attack the weakest part of the body first. And we are constantly bombarded by sources of stress. Even the noise of air rushing through a partly opened car window can produce enough stress to raise your blood pressure by as much as 10 points. There is no way to avoid stress completely.

The problem then is not avoiding stress but coping with and understanding it. The triggers of stress are not the essential causes of stress. People will say that they are stressed because of financial problems, marital discord or job pressures. Those are stress triggers and there are thousands of them. The crucial issue, however, is not the triggers, but how we respond to them, how much actual control we have over them, that will determine the harmful effects on the body psychosomatically.

But there is a major difference between stress and distress. Stress is not destructive in and of itself. In fact, we need it as we need wind to move a sailboat. Distress, on the other hand is destructive like a gale-force wind that forces us to haul in the sails or perish. You can't utilize the winds of a gale to propel the boat — you must wait it out. The controlled response to the trigger effect is what keeps stress from becoming distress.

Distress inevitably occurs even in the most self-controlled individual. We need to know how to deal with it, almost as an emergency kind of response.

Jesus suffered stress when the people wanted to stone Him and throw Him off a cliff. He had many enemies and was often placed in a position of having to defend Himself. In the Garden of Gethsemane He suffered great agony of soul. In Luke's gospel, it is referred to as "great distress." He suffered psychosomatically to the point that he sweat blood.

Have you ever known anyone who has literally sweat blood? This phenomenon is produced today only in extreme cases of very deep hypnosis, and then only a slight bleeding occurs. Yet this holy writer said the drops of blood from Jesus fell to the ground. It must have been a profuse kind of sweating of blood. The mind of Jesus, in realizing not only His future sufferings, the scourging and the crucifixion, but the heinousness of sin and its effect on mankind, caused the sweating of blood.

What did our Lord do in this emergency situation? He had moved from stress to distress, so He prayed! Luke 22:43 says an angel appeared in response to his prayer and *comforted* Him. He did not attempt to deal with the agonizing distress through His own human willpower alone. Jesus called upon His Heavenly Father to help Him. And God sent a messenger in response to that prayer, subdued the distress and comforted Him.

We can learn much about stress, and the peace of God to banish it, from Scripture. Let's first look at some of the psychological factors. Dr. Albert Ellis, the famous psychologist, when asked what he thought was his greatest achievement in life, replied, "Every single day for the past 40 years, I have resolved to be pigheadedly undepressed. Any emotional misery is the result of either ignorance or stupidity. I refuse to have either label applied to myself and I have taught this to my patients."

We are either ignorant of how to deal with the situation or are stupid in refusing to deal with it. We have some control over our emotions; we also have external help available in God's divine power, qualified counselors and others experts in the field. *Something can be done about emotional misery.* Ignorance and stupidity can be removed. *No one can ever disturb you emotionally unless you allow yourself to be disturbed.*

Seneca said the same thing long ago. He said that if you are disturbed by other people that cause you ongoing anxiety — stress response — you deserve to be upset for being so foolish as to allow yourself to be upset. A centuries-old observation!

That does not mean we have an absolute positive

control. It takes a very well integrated, highly mature personality to have that kind of control. One of the most stressful moments of my life comes every time I step up to a podium, and I do it often in the course of a year.

There was a five-year study of stress conducted by Dr. Jay Segal at Temple University. He found that 90 percent of all anxiety, frustration and other stress reactions can be placed into five causative categories. The important thing to remember is not *what* caused the stress but *why* we reacted to it the way we did.

The first of the five weaknesses within ourselves that allow us to be hurt by stress is *vulnerability*. Vulnerable individuals have lost internal control, such as persons recently divorced. They are plagued with feelings of guilt and failure. Sometimes it is a person who turns against someone else and blames their upset condition on someone else's actions (Sirach 28:11). They plead innocence because they "had no other choice." It is an emotional rather than an intellectual response to events and circumstances (cf. Ecclesiastes 10:4).

The second category is *demandingness*. Some individuals are perfectionists. They demand to know why someone else can't do something right. "Why do you have to flick your cigarette ashes on the floor?" "Why can't you put your toothbrush back exactly where you found it?" It must be done their way; there is little room for compromise. Resistance from others only compounds the tension (cf. Proberbs 30:32-33).

The third category of responses is *fear* or *anxiety*. There is the story of the patient who ran out of the operating room and fled down the hospital corridor. He ran into an intern who wanted to know why he was running from the operating room.

"Because that nurse in there was saying not to worry, that an appendectomy is a very simple operation!"

"So?" said the intern, not comprehending. "Why run away?"

"Because," replied the fearful patient, "she wasn't talking to me, she was talking to the surgeon!"

Fear and anxiety cause the "runaway" response, a

reluctance to face and experience one's fears objectively. Such persons will say they do not want to take on a new position unless they can do an A-1 job. Or they may avoid meeting new people for fear they will not make a good impression. They deal with life's problems by anxiety-producing avoidance (cf. Proverbs 28:12).

Fourth, is a response I call *awfulizing*, an attitude that regards situations as "awful" or "deplorable." "I'll *never* make it through this week" or "I'll *never* recuperate from this divorce." Gideon was an "awfulizer" (Judges 6).

Fifth, is *judgmentalness*. Know-it-alls think they can judge others or themselves, but are often wrong. "I'm just no good" or "Did you see that crazy driver? That's the kind of animal we have running around the streets these days." It is usually a universal judgment passed by persons living under extreme stress. Such opinionated people ultimately appear foolish (Proverbs 28:26).

Spiritually, we can see what is at issue here: the need for charity, patience and fortitude. Psychologically, the need is to reverse emotional deterioration. It is less obvious but equally true that the spiritual virtues could provide solutions for most of the psychological defects.

A survey of 2,500 Americans conducted by Dr. Philip Shaver, professor of psychology at the University of Denver, found that the greater a person's religious conviction and belief in God's love, the more likely he or she was to be healthy in mind and body. The more a person surrenders to God in quiet prayer, the more health that person will have physically and emotionally. This approach is worth considering, since according to some estimates, 80 to 90 percent of all hospital beds are filled with individuals whose illnesses are at least partially psychosomatic.

Dr. Richard Procton, Wake Forest University, says that belief in God, if it really carries with it conviction and reliance upon God, actually increases one's life span. The book of Proverbs reaffirms this (Proverbs 3:2). You are healthier when you trust and obey the Lord, and days will be added to your life (cf. Deuteronomy 25:15).

Dr. Neil Warren, dean of the graduate school of psychology at Fuller Theological Seminary, says that virtually all research supports the fact that if you possess a strong religious belief, you are not as prone to stress and tension as one who is less religious. Statistically, he continues, truly religious persons, as a category, drink less, smoke less, divorce less and experience less violence in their homes. A truly religious person simply has a different behavior pattern (II Corinthians 5:17; Ephesians 4:23; 5:8).

Once we are truly walking with the Lord, we are "equipped to do all good things" (Ephesians 4:12). So often, however, we do not use that equipment. The deeper our spiritual life, the better equipped we are to practice self-control, which includes the ability to prevent our stress from becoming distress. To get that equipment we must go to Jesus who invites us (Matthew 11:28): "Come to me all you who labor and are burdened (full of stress) and *I* will give you rest (peace)." The art of making peace with stress is acquired by simply responding to this gentle invitation from the Heart of Jesus.

This is Christic peace. Just as Jesus speaks of abiding in *His* love, of receiving *His* joy, He also speaks of giving us *His* peace (John 14:27). Only the truly Spirit-filled person grasps what that means existentially (I Corinthians 2:12). These are just words to others, but for a person close to Christ, it is very meaningful that He would extend His peace to us.

In Scripture, we find stress, the antithesis of peace, spoken of in three terms. All stress is either *pressure*, *strain* or *tension*. Pressure comes when we feel our world is falling in on us, that we are being pushed from every side; strain is the struggle of reaching for a goal, climbing the ladder of success; tension is the pulling apart, being torn in different directions. While Scripture refers to these three forms of stress, it also provides antidotes for each:

Acts 14:22 speaks of *pressure*: "We enter the kingdom of God through many tribulations and stresses." But

Romans 8:35 reminds us that no trouble or stress is able to keep us from the love of God. Romans 12:12 tells us to be patient in the midst of our troubles and stresses. Scripture is replete with advice on handling pressure.

We see *strain* referred to I Thessalonians 1:3 in the striving for, looking for, eagerly awaiting the second coming of Christ. We see it, too, in II Corinthians 6 where Paul speaks of his troubles of shipwreck, lynch mobs and staying awake at night watching — the fear and anxiety of physical threats and persecution. As a delayed palliative, he invites open-hearted sympathy (verse 13).

Tension is portrayed all through II Corinthians 4 and Romans 7, the inner striving that imbalances us. For all these, Jesus alone is the answer, along with the realization that the conflict is brief, compared to the eternal reward it brings (II Corinthians 4:17).

Scripture provides a program for coping with stress. To make peace with stress, we must have a very personal knowledge of and commitment to the Lord Jesus. To just go through the motions of Christianity, attend church on Sunday and view Christ as an historical figure from 2,000 years ago, will not do it. St. Thomas Aquinas spoke of the importance of personally *appropriating* salvation as the effect of redemption through Christ. "To as many as *received* him, to them Jesus gave the power to become the sons of God" (John 1:12). We must *embrace* Him.

This relationship is one of love. Where there is love, there is a spinoff experience called trust. Psalm 32:10 says, "Many sorrows and stresses and tribulations come to the wicked, but *abiding love surrounds those who trust in the Lord.*" That's why the psalmist could say in at least 10 places, "The Lord is my shield." Christians are shielded from the impact of these things; there is a definite protection.

The psalmist goes on to say (Psalm 32:11), "So rejoice all of you who are his" — who belong to Him in total commitment — "and shout for joy all those who struggle to obey him."

Psalm 34:18-19 says, "The Lord is close to those whose hearts are breaking; he rescues those who are humbly sorry for their sins. The good man does not totally escape all troubles (stress). He has them too, but the Lord helps him in each and every one." The same reminder of God's availability during stress can be found in Psalm 50:15 and 121:7 and many other places.

I like especially Psalm 112:6-8: "Such a man will not be overthrown by adverse circumstances. God's constant care of him will make a deep impression upon all who see it. Such a man does not fear bad news nor does he live in dread of what may happen, for he is settled in his mind that Jehovah God will take care of him, and that is why he is not afraid but can calmly face his adversaries."

And Philippians 4:6-7: "Be not anxious about anything, but pray about everything. By prayer and supplication and thanksgiving *let your requests be made known to God* (notice, no anxiety or petulance), and then the peace of God which passes all understanding will keep your hearts (affections) and minds (thoughts) in Christ Jesus."

Imagine two small boys, one of whom is a spoiled brat, the other a "good kid." They're walking down the beach with their dads and decide they want an ice cream cone. The first child yells and demands an ice cream cone. His father says it will spoil his dinner and he can't have it right then. An altercation ensues. The child is full of anxiety expressed in his pressured petition.

The other child says, "Daddy, can I have an ice cream cone?" The father replies, "Let's wait until after dinner and then we'll have one. That way you won't spoil your appetite. Would that be okay?" The good kid agrees and they return after supper and have their ice cream cones. The difference between the two cases is obvious: one asked petulantly with anxiety, the other calmly presented the desire. Both youngsters had the same petition, but one was expressed stressfully, and the other calmly. Anxiety-free (i.e. stress-free) petition, as Paul urges (Philippians 4:6) leads to peace (verse 7).

When we "present our needs to the Lord," we should do so *calmly*, Matthew 6:8 tells us, "Your heavenly Father knows you have need of all these things . . ." so you don't need to convince Him by anguished whining. He wants you to ask and receive, but to do so without anxiety.

To pray with anxiety in your soul shows lack of perfect acquiescence to God's will, and may even indicate a resistance to God's will. We may not want to face the fact that we are at variance with God's will, but think about it for a moment. We have to do some very deep soul-searching to see how much we are flowing with the movement of God. Isaiah (48 and 66) speaks of peace *flowing* like a river. Peace is not a stagnant thing, it's moving, flowing. When the petition flows in the direction of His will, there's nothing trying to dam up the flow of God's providence, and His peace becomes ours, flowing together like two rivers merging in confluence.

We have to constantly "pull up our socks" to prevent ourselves from slipping back into worry and anxiety. Here are some practical suggestions for dealing with anxiety:

1. Try doing one thing at a time.

2. Try to enjoy what you do — not always an easy task. If your job is drudgery, you're sick and tired of housekeeping, you're fed up fighting traffic, it's not easy to enjoy things which in and of themselves tend to be anxiety-producing. Colossians 3:23 says, "Whatever you do, do it heartily as for the Lord and not for men." Are you working ultimately for the boss or for the Lord? Lift your sights higher to ease work-related stress.

3. Be sure you are well organized. A sense of orderliness in itself gives a sense of security. The result of disorderliness is often procrastination, which can lead to accumulated pressure and stress.

4. Change (i.e. improve) what you can, but realize what things you *cannot* change. Much of our lack of serenity and peace comes precisely because we do

not realize what we can and can't change with God's help. *"Pray, sailor, but row for shore!"*

5. And lastly, look for a picture of yourself in this doleful ditty:

As children bring their broken toys with tears for us to mend,
I brought my broken dreams to God because he was my friend;
But then instead of leaving Him in peace to work alone,
I hung around and tried to help with ways that were my own.
At last I snatched them back and cried, "How can you be so slow?"
"My child," He said, "what could I do? You never did let go!"

Taking a Second Look at Christ's Comfort: Making Peace With Stress

Ask Yourself (Or discuss with a study group) . . .

1. In what ways is stress unavoidable?

2. The things that trigger stress are not the real problem. What is?

3. What are the differences between stress and distress? Did Jesus ever experience either, or both?

4. How did Jesus handle an "emergency" situation?

5. Whose fault usually is it when we become disturbed? Why?

6. What five basic weaknesses within ourselves allow us to be hurt by stress?

7. What proof do we have that deep reliance upon God increases one's lifespan?

8. Are Christians shielded from hurtful things or the impact of hurtful things? Discuss.

9. Discuss some practical ways of dealing with anxiety. Use Scripture to help you make your point.

Co-author Clint Kelly is a teacher, author, journalist and publisher whose articles have appeared in dozens of secular and religious periodicals as diverse as *Charisma, Family Circle,* and *American History Illustrated.* Mr. Kelly lives with his wife and four children in Everett, Washington.

As a follow-up study of various dimensions of inner peace, cognate to what has been dealt with in this book, the reader is referred to the author's other books, especially *"Faith: Key To The Heart Of God"*, or to some or all of the following cassette tapes by the author. (Other tape titles also are listed in his free tape catalog, available on request).

"How To Cope" (2 tapes)

"Coping With Worry" (2 tapes)

"Achieving Inner Peace" (4 tapes)

"Rooted In Faith" (4 tapes)

"Getting Close To God" (2 tapes)

"Healing Of Memories — Long Form" (6 tapes)

"Healing of Memories — Short Form" (2 tapes)

"God's Love In Your Life" (2 tapes)

"The God-Encounter Experience" (1 tape)

"In Search Of God's Will" (4 tapes)

"Guide Through Darkness' (4 tapes)

"The Why of Suffering" (1 tape)

"God's-Eye-View of Suffering" (2 tapes)

"Discerning The Will Of God" (2 Tapes)

"Healing The Family Tree" (4 tapes)

Ordering information:

    Single tape (approx. 1½ hours): $5

    2-tape albums (approx. 3 hours): $10

    4-tape albums (approx. 6 hours): $18

    6-tape albums (approx. 9 hours): $28

Please enclose payment with order (U.S. funds only), adding 10% for postage and handling. California residents add 6½% tax. 30-day replacement warranty for defective tapes. Prices subject to change.

Order tapes and books from:

CLARETIAN TAPE MINISTRY
P.O. Box 19100
Los Angeles, CA 90019
Phone: (213) 734-1234

192